What's Fair?

Media Studies Series

The Problem of
Equity in Journalism

What's Fair?

Robert Giles & Robert W. Snyder
editors

Transaction Publishers
New Brunswick (U.S.A.) and London (U.K.)

Library of Congress Catalog Number: 99- 11505
ISBN: 0-7658-0616-9
Printed in the United States of America

Library of Congress Cataloging-in-Publication Data

What's fair? : the problem of equity in journalism / edited by Robert Giles
and Robert Snyder.
    p. cm. — (Media studies series)
Originally published in the Media studies journal, winter 1998.
Includes bibliographical references and index.
ISBN 0-7658-0616-9 (alk. paper)
    1. Journalistic ethics. 2. Press and politics. 3. Freedom of the press.
I. Giles, Robert H., 1933– . II. Snyder, Robert W., 1955– . III. Series.
PN4756.W53   1999
174'.9097—dc21   99-11505
                                                             CIP

Contents

"To ask a former newspaper editor to fess up and re-examine acts of unfairness during his years on the clock is both therapeutic and humiliating," writes a retired editor. "Why not start with my most blatantly irresponsible, stupid and unfair performance as an editor."

A media critic who criticized the use of unnamed sources reflects on what he learned when he looked at some of his old stories. "Oh, I hadn't sprinkled 'reliable sources' and 'knowledgeable sources' and unnamed 'top newspaper executives' throughout my stories with careless abandon. But neither had I been nearly as vigilant as I had thought."

A television correspondent recalls one of the greatest challenges of covering the White House in an era of multimedia and a 24-hour news cycle: "I want a viewer to take what I have distilled into a one-minute 30-second story and come away with the same impression of the facts that I came to after hours, even days of reporting."

An editor recalls a lesson he learned as an investigative reporter: "[I]f I could choose whether I'd be known as honest, fair or accurate, I'd like to be known as fair. I also want to be honest and accurate, of course, but mainly I want to be fair."

"The anger about Clinton that drives my writing has nothing to do with his sexual trysts or even about the corruption among a good many of his cabinet members whom he, after all, appointed," writes a columnist." My "special interest" as a journalist and citizen (there is no separating the two) is the Constitution. And no president in American history has done more diversified damage to the Constitution than Clinton."

A BBC correspondent recalls lessons learned when he failed to live up to BBC standards of fairness: "[H]ate figures demand of us an extra sensitivity, a greater commitment to fairness. One may well ultimately reach the same conclusion as the partisan reporter, but at least it will be based on knowledge and inquiry."

A newspaper editor recalls what happened when the Socialist Party asked why she never printed the number of votes they received in elections: "After thinking it over, it became obvious to me that the fairness I was so fond of extended only to those who won or came in second. I had never even entertained the possibility of covering minor-party candidates, either during the campaign or in the election results."

"For five years, on a regular basis, I fought the more extreme attempts by my editors at the BBC back in Britain to portray America as a land full of gun-toting, bible-bashing, collagen-filled lunatics," recalls a former correspondent. "In essence, they sought to have their (oh so British) prejudices about Yanks confirmed."

Part 2: Fairness—A History

"American journalists, buffeted by critics from every corner and wracked by self-criticism too, have long insisted that they try to be fair," writes an analyst of media history. "But what's fair? That has changed from one era to the next."

"At many moments in American history journalists have been accused of unfairness and abuse of power," writes a communications scholar. "We are living today in one such moment. It is, perhaps, particularly painful to journalists, because it follows an unusual period during which the prestige of the news media was extremely high."

"The Hutchins Commission on Freedom of the Press was that bunch of pointy-heads who threatened to sic the government on the press if it didn't behave itself—right?" asks a journalist and historian. "Wrong."

"The first time I read the Hutchins Commission report, it was like reading Plato on journalism—a philosophical framework to the craft," writes a former editor and publisher who put the report into practice at his paper. "The ideas raised by the Commission are relevant and worth trying in a time when readers, viewers and citizens all ask, 'What are the standards of journalism? What does good journalism look like?'"

A First Amendment scholar and university president assays the Hutchins report some 50 years after its publication: "The report's articulate denunciation of the media's increasing pandering to the baser desires of the population and its depiction of the media's noble role in a democratic society give it, in my view, the potential to be an enduring document."

"Even the worst individual case of unfairness does not approach the level of injustice being perpetrated by the information industry as a whole," writes a former political writer and editor. "What could be more unfair to citizens than the outright corruption of journalism, which takes place daily in all quarters of the so-called news media?"

At first glance, it may appear that political talk radio has been usurped by talk about relationships and preadolescent humor. However, a sense of absolutism and outrage still dominates the airwaves.

"In Britain," writes a legal scholar, "a battle over fairness regulation is looming in a media landscape defined by digitally converged media, consolidation of ownership and international broadcasting. At stake is not only a tradition of fairness bequeathed by the history of the British Broadcasting Corporation, but the very structure and rationales of British media regulations."

An authority on media law reports on how a television station licensed in London that produces programming in Belgium for Kurdish viewers in the Middle East was fined for fairness violations by a British regulatory authority.

Part 3: Fairness—A Goal

"Journalists ought to ask difficult questions of public officials," writes an Indiana congressman. "Whether they ask these questions in a combative or dispassionate manner is not really all that important. What is important is whether they listen to the answers."

A philosopher and journalist contemplates his two professions and concludes, "What journalists consider fair—or fair-minded—and what philosophers think about the topic, is so galactically distant from each other as to require NASA-enhanced communication between parties."

"In covering Northern Ireland, journalists face painful dilemmas," writes a Belfast magazine editor. "Imagine yourself a reporter who possesses facts that, if published, could undermine politicians who might make a historic compromise with sworn enemies. Do you publish and damn the consequences?"

"You can kill with words; this is the poisonous charm of a journalist's work," writes a former Polish dissident turned newspaper editor. "But one can also do good with words: One can disenchant totalitarian enchantment; one can teach tolerance; one can give testimony to truth and freedom. Struggle with your pen, but struggle in a decent way, without hatred."

"Fairness up to the limits of the endurable was the very bedrock of Murray Kempton's journalism," writes a colleague of the late columnist. "The great grandson of an Episcopal bishop, he worked from a firm moral center, carefully weighing such facts and characters as he encountered against a personal standard of ethics more immutable than that of the courts and certainly of journalism."

"What was it about Tony Lukas that prompted people to peel away layer after layer of memory while his tape recorder hummed quietly?" ask two people whom the author and reporter profiled in his book *Common Ground*. "We suspect that it was Tony's own struggle that gave us permission to share ours; his own vulnerability reassured ours."

Six editors reflect on what happened when they wound up in the news.

"Journalists wrestle daily with the questions that occupy ethicists and theologians," writes an ethicist who has taught journalism students. "All of them struggle to give order and meaning to the endless and confusing flow of human experience. If they acknowledge their common purpose, they will have much to teach each other."

Preface

What's fair? It's an old question in journalism, but in 1998 it seems more difficult to answer than ever. The cycle of story, spin and counterspin that surrounds the White House is only the most obvious part of the problem.

In the past twenty-five years or so, as communications scholar Daniel Hallin reminds us, the practice of journalism has changed enormously—particularly in the United States. The demarcation of public and private life that once ruled certain kinds of stories out of bounds has eroded, leaving reporters with the unenviable challenge of having to cover events whose seaminess inevitably taints all who touch them. Old certainties that gave credibility to journalists, such as trust in government sources, have broken down—weakening the authority of journalists as well. Commercial pressures, and a tidal wave of information and entertainment media, have engulfed the news business—leaving the definitions of journalism and journalistic standards vague and uncertain. And the technology of news reporting is speeding up news cycles in ways that leave little time for sober and measured judgments.

We don't pretend to have all the answers on what's fair in journalism. But we do believe that this issue of the *Journal* can advance a conversation that will take us closer to establishing a better understanding of what fairness in journalism means in theory and in practice.

Too many discussions of fairness are either numbingly abstract or impossibly righteous. To avoid those hazards, we have grounded this issue in stories—the kind of stories journalists tell each other and the kind of stories people tell about journalism. We hope that these will spark compelling questions and ideas that will generate an energetic conversation about journalism and its place in our time.

In part 1, "Fairness—A Struggle," journalists explore a subject that they normally share only with close friends and colleagues—their own efforts to be fair, including their failures. "Where in God's name do I begin?" asks Thomas Winship, former editor of *The Boston Globe*.

"To ask a former newspaper editor to fess up and re-examine acts of unfairness during his years on the clock is both therapeutic and humiliating." And edifying. In exploring struggles with fairness that occurred in places as different as South Africa, Washington and the South Bronx, our contributors share what they learned in meditating on issues of fairness in their own work. They have much to teach us.

If journalists and people who care about journalism are confused about the question of fairness, we can get oriented by taking a look backward to see how we got where we are today. In part 2, "Fairness— A History," nine contributors examine the history of the fairness question. "Today's journalistic fairness in the United States is a blend of high hopes, historic traditions, contemporary political culture and the expediencies journalists face in keeping audiences, owners and sources at bay," writes Michael Schudson, an analyst of media history. "It is a shifting set of principles and practices that will be tested and reformulated by a changing informational environment whose shape will not hold still." The section includes a collection of essays analyzing a notable effort to establish a set of guiding principles for the American media—the Hutchins Commission report of 1947, which is evaluated here by a historian, a journalist and a First Amendment authority. In a comparative vein, two authorities on international communications law examine British regulations for fairness in broadcasting at the end of the 20th century.

In part 3, "Fairness—A Goal," our contributors explore what struggles for fairness mean in a variety of contexts, from American newsrooms to post-Communist Poland to Northern Ireland. Adam Michnik of Poland, who has made the journey from dissident essayist to above-ground newspaper editor, admonishes his fellow journalists: "Struggle with your pen, but struggle in a decent way, without hatred. Do not hit more than is needed. Do not think you have a prescription for being just."

In closing, in our book review essay, ethicist Donald Shriver reviews four works on journalism ethics. He concludes that journalism, religion and media ethics, in their efforts to make sense of events and distinguish events of greater and lesser importance, all have much in common. "Reason meets religion—and journalism," Shriver writes, "at the place where some 'ultimate concern,' in theologian Paul Tillich's phrase, searches the sky for a north star."

One of our ultimate concerns is for journalism that is free yet fair, probing yet credible and authoritative in content yet open to many voices. We believe that the essays in this volume advance all of those goals.

The Editors

Part 1

Fairness—A Struggle

1

Obvious Lessons in Hindsight

Thomas Winship

Where in God's name do I begin? To ask a former newspaper editor to fess up and re-examine acts of unfairness during his years on the clock is both therapeutic and humiliating. Why not start with my most blatantly irresponsible, stupid and unfair performance as an editor.

The scene: *The Boston Globe* city room, presidential election night, 1960. Kennedy vs. Nixon. I was the youngish managing editor, cutting my teeth as CEO on my first national election. At 9:30 p.m. I approved the banner headline for the first edition, "Kennedy Wins Big." About midnight, the paper was on the street. It made the network news reports only because the *Globe* was telling the world something nobody else was prepared to report. The Kennedy camp in Hyannis was jubilant.

Toward 2 a.m. the race tightened, turned into a dead heat. Wiser heads in the newsroom questioned our first edition headline. For the main edition, with a 2 a.m. deadline, we scaled back and removed "Big" from the headline. So, it was "Kennedy Wins."

With that, at 2:10 a.m., Bob Healy, our political editor and columnist, and I put on our fedoras and headed out to Cambridge to join the victory celebration at Arthur M. Schlesinger Jr.'s house. Half the would-be New Frontier gang was gathered there to watch the returns—the McGeorge Bundys, Galbraiths, Archibalds, Coxes, Chayses, etc., etc.

What an appropriate way to climax our years of intense coverage of the local hero's race for the White House, we thought. As we approached the house, Healy noticed a Stevenson-for-President poster in an up-stairs window (Arthur's wife Marian was a holdout Adlai partisan).

When we walked into Schlesinger's rambling Irving Street house, we were met by silence, glum faces, heavy smoking and anxious anger.

All those Washington-bound academics were in shock. Everything pointed to a crap shoot.

So, what did I do? Whoever heard of a Kennedy losing? He will pull it out, I mused. I phoned the office from Cambridge and told the desk, "We've hung tough this long, stay with our head," I ordered. "Kennedy Wins" was the headline through all morning editions. I eventually went home and slept like a baby.

Breakfast the next day was no fun as I wondered whether I'd be looking for a new job. Fortunately, for the *Globe*'s sake, we still had an evening paper, which maintained its sanity and wrote headlines off the news instead of off a stupid editor's hunch.

If Kennedy had not snaked out his eventual 17,000 vote victory, that *Boston Globe* headline "Kennedy Wins" would have gone down in newspaper history, along with the *Chicago Tribune*'s immortal "Dewey Beats Truman" banner. Two examples of overexuberant editing.

My face is still red over my cavalier performance that night.

Why did I do it? Because Bob Healy and I undoubtedly had become too preoccupied by Kennedy's four-year campaign for the White House and too close to the Kennedy gang. Kennedy, after all, was the first serious, local presidential candidate since Cal Coolidge. It was a giant story, and we had given it saturation coverage—the warts and all, but damn few of them. We'd seen him pull out of close calls before. And by golly, he would this time, we were convinced.

Sure, we wanted the hometown hero to win. His candidacy put the *Globe* in the big leagues. We had the big-shot political writers of the national press taking note of what the *Globe* said. Those are the reasons why I stayed with that reckless headline.

The obvious lesson: Don't get too close to political candidates. It's addictive, and you always get hurt before you take the cure.

Another act of unfairness and stupidity that will forever haunt me is a decision I made during the tense days of the school busing crises in Boston in the mid 1970s.

During the desegregation crisis, our paper was the dominant public voice in the area. The *Globe* became almost as much of a central player as federal Judge Arthur W. Garrity Jr., who ordered the busing.

The editorial page, under the unflappable direction of Anne Wyman, held to its pro-integration, hence pro-busing position, much to the exasperation of probably the majority of the public and the paper's own employees.

It soon became clear that our staff columnists, on both sides of the issue, drew the most fire—far more than the news coverage did. At this point I told the columnists that the school issue was an off-limits subject until further notice. My rationale was fear of inciting more community violence.

I enforced the ban for about two weeks. The town did not blow up, for which everyone was grateful.

Yet to this day I have been plagued by my censorship of the paper's columnists. Short of unquestionably endangering human life, is there ever an excuse for censoring columnists, except for very bad taste? I think not. I'm ashamed of myself.

In those wrenching days of community hatred, the *Globe* was pilloried by busing opponents. Eleven rifle shots were fired into the building, tacks were strewn in the paper loading area, and a delivery truck was dumped into the South Boston Harbor.

In retrospect, I wish we had objected more vigorously to certain aspects of the desegregation plan. Under the plan, Roxbury's black children were bused into South Boston schools, and Southie's white kids were sent to Roxbury. That was an unnecessary and inflammatory burden to inflict upon both neighborhoods. We also should have fought harder for suburban involvement in the desegregation effort. Yet our coverage and editorializing were rock solid, good enough to win the Pulitzer Prize for Public Service that year. Credit for the news coverage goes 100 percent to ex-*New York Times* news editor Robert Phelps, then the *Globe*'s assistant managing editor for metropolitan news.

In hindsight, I don't regret for one moment the broad editorial position we took—100 percent support of the Supreme Court's integration decree. We stood by the locally drafted implementation order in spite of its flawed busing features.

Why didn't we question more vigorously the details of the busing plan? I think we became overwhelmed by the street demonstrations and the opposition assaults on the paper.

I suppose the lesson I learned is that in times of a continuing breaking story, editors should stand back, take a deep breath and reassess their paper's overall position in the community before it is too late to dig deeper.

My final confession goes to the heart of a paper's relationship to its readers. For many years as editor, I also directed the editorial and op-ed pages. About eight or 10 years before I quit, I gradually became an advocate of the so-called separation-of-church-and-state management style—the system under which the editor only worries about news coverage, while the editor of the editorial page oversees the editorial and op-ed pages. Both editors report to the publisher, and it's forbidden for either editor to second-guess the other.

No single incident prompted my move. I relinquished my hold over the editorial side for several reasons. I thought it would be good for the publisher to involve himself more in the nonbusiness aspects of his paper. I was impressed, too, that *The New York Times*, *The Washington Post* and *The Wall Street Journal* were all church and staters. On the make those days, I thought these premier papers could do no wrong. Even more important, the incoming editorial page editor wanted more independence from me and thought he would get it by reporting to the publisher instead of me. Under either system, the publisher, of course, retains ultimate control.

I do believe in the "separation" system for national newspapers because of the inordinate public pressure those papers come under and the influence they enjoy. Not so for the big regionals and the community dailies, in my opinion. I still think it is unwise for the regionals to set up this artificial barrier between editors.

Another point. When a newspaper is involved in a major investigative series or a community initiative, the two ranking editors may differ on the worth of the project. As a result, the public gets a blurred picture of the paper's stand.

It's worth noting that the church-state concept so nurtured by the *Times-Post-Journal* axis has not exactly swept the newspaper world. You can count the number of "separatist" newspapers on one hand. Why is it any healthier to turn the daily direction of the editorials over to the business side than to the news side? I say, let editors be editors and publishers be publishers.

Thomas Winship, a 1985–86 inaugural Media Studies Center fellow, is chairman of the International Center for Journalists and a columnist for Editor & Publisher. *He is the former editor of* The Boston Globe.

2

Off the Record, Off the Mark

David Shaw

It was a shocking—and embarrassing—discovery. I was sitting at
the kitchen table one morning in the summer of 1983, reading through
a dozen or so of the series of articles that I had written for the *Los
Angeles Times* over the previous seven years. An editor at a New York
publishing house had seen an earlier book-length collection of my stories on the American news media, and he had offered me a contract for
a second collection. But newspaper stories tend not to have a great
shelf life, and I wasn't yet sure if I had enough that would stand up for
a hardcover edition. If I did, though, I knew one story that I would
definitely include—a two-part series I'd written two years earlier on
the dangers inherent in the media's increasing use of unnamed sources.

I've always felt strongly that we owe it to our readers to tell them
exactly who our sources are whenever possible. Otherwise, as I had
written in that series, "'Sources,' under the protective cloak of anonymity, are permitted to use the press for personal and political purposes—to grind axes, advance ambitions, attack rivals and mislead the
public." When I reread this particular series to try to determine how
best to turn it—like my other multipart series—into a single book chapter, I remembered that in writing it originally I had been determined to
practice what I preached. The series contained not a single unnamed
source.

But now I was rereading several series I had written before that one,
looking for anything that might be worthy of inclusion in a book. I was
horrified. I knew that I had occasionally used unnamed sources myself
in various stories throughout my career. As any reporter will tell you—
especially anyone who's covered those two bastions of backstabbing,

Washington and Hollywood—there are times when you just can't get the information you need unless you promise not to reveal your source's name. But because of my visceral resistance to the practice, I had assumed that I'd always been extremely careful—indeed downright niggardly—about using unnamed sources.

Wrong.

Oh, I hadn't sprinkled "reliable sources" and "knowledgeable sources" and unnamed "top newspaper executives" throughout my stories with careless abandon. But neither had I been nearly as vigilant as I had thought. I couldn't remember the exact circumstances of every interview, of course, so I went back to my original interview notes on many of the anonymous quotes I'd used, and I concluded that in most cases, I'd been—in a word—lazy. The vast majority of the time, it seemed to me, there was no compelling reason for my source to have demanded anonymity and certainly no legitimate reason for my having granted it.

I was mortified—and I vowed then and there not to use another anonymous source unless (a) the information was absolutely, positively, incontrovertibly essential to an important story and (b) I had tried every form of personal, professional and moral persuasion I could to induce the source to go on the record.

I made that kitchen-table promise to myself almost 15 years ago, and I'm fairly confident that if the old National League pitcher Mordecai "Three Finger" Brown were alive today, he could do a Nexis search of every story I've written since then and be able to count on the fingers of his right hand the number of unnamed sources I've used. In fact, he'd probably have a finger or two left over—even though almost every story I write has quotes from journalists being critical of their own colleagues and competitors and even, at times, their bosses.

I don't say this to be boastful. I'm far more ashamed of my earlier use of unnamed sources than I am proud of my more recent vigilance. But I do wish more reporters would take the extra effort to get their sources on the record. As I said earlier, I realize this is not always possible. As we've all learned, though—most recently in the Bill Clinton/Monica Lewinsky coverage—using unnamed sources is a deadly virus in the body politic (and in the body journalistic). Virtually every major "new" angle in the Clinton/Lewinsky *scandale* has been based on an unnamed source—the (allegedly) semen-stained dress, the grand jury testimony, the various comments attributed to people close to Clinton (a valet, Secret Service agents, his friends and aides). Most of them have turned out to be false or remain, at best, unproven. And yet, they've led the nation's best newspapers, the nightly network newscasts and the weekly newsmagazines.

Some journalists seem to feel that if they have *two* unnamed sources, it automatically validates a story. I've heard many reporters speak of the "two-source" rule as if it were either a clause in an insurance policy or one of the Ten Commandments. But I don't think readers necessarily accept this. The overuse of unnamed sources is probably the single biggest complaint I hear about the media from people outside the profession—bigger even than bias, sensationalism and inaccuracy. And when I tell nonjournalists that reputable reporters usually insist on two sources before they'll use something without attribution, they are not impressed.

Every reporter worth his weight in tape cassettes knows that once you have one source telling you something, it's usually pretty easy to wangle an "independent," anonymous confirmation out of a second source. Early in the Clinton/Lewinsky story, for example, the on-line edition of *The Dallas Morning News* reported that a Secret Service agent had seen the two of them in a "compromising position." Editors at the *Morning News* thought they had two independent sources for the story, thus meeting their standard. But after the story appeared, the first source said the information was not accurate, and when it turned out that the "second source" had no firsthand knowledge of the alleged incident, the *Morning News* pulled the story and replaced it with a more tentative version. The second source had simply confirmed what the *Morning News* already had—sort of—by declining to wave the reporter off the story, says Ralph Langer, editor of the paper. "It was one of those 'Will I destroy my career if I go with this story?' kind of questions," Langer says, "and the source said 'No.'"

There's no question that the accelerated news cycle and the absence of standards and gatekeepers in cyberspace have both expanded the use of unnamed sources and exacerbated its consequences. Who has time to think—let alone try to talk someone into going on the record or, failing that, to find, cultivate and persuade a second or third or fourth source to go on the record—when Matt Drudge (or someone else of his ilk) is already on-line with the latest unconfirmed, unreliable rumor from the most clever (or most available) unnamed source?

When I began being rigid about the use of unnamed sources, I devised a simple technique. If a source asks to go off the record, I try briefly to keep him on the record. If he resists, I relent—"on one condition," I always say: "When I've actually written my story, I want to call you and read your quotes to you and try to persuade you to go on the record. It will still be your decision. But I want you to agree to at least take my call and consider my arguments." In fifteen years, I've never had a source refuse that deal. And in fifteen years, I've only had one source reject my subsequent argument and insist on anonymity. In that case, I threw out the quote rather than use it anonymously.

I understand that writing a breaking news story on deadline is considerably different from writing the kind of long-term, reflective stories I do. A reporter on a hotly competitive daily story generally doesn't have the luxury of calling a source back several days—or, in my case, sometimes several weeks—later to discuss attribution in a calm, reasoned fashion. But the rush to be first is the enemy of accuracy. On most stories, we're only satisfying our individual and institutional egos. Do we really think our readers give a damn whether we report a story before another newspaper or a television station or a Web site? Obviously, I'm not suggesting we delay our stories indefinitely; that would be history, not daily journalism. But I'd be hard-pressed to think of many stories on which the public would be harmed if we delayed a day or two to be sure our facts are correct and our quotes are attributed. Unfortunately, too many reporters feel a greater loyalty to their sources than to their readers—and a greater desire to impress their peers than to serve the public.

The bottom line is that for all their insistence that the Republic might collapse if we couldn't rely on our Deep Throats, too many reporters too often use too many unnamed sources—not because they have to but because they can and because they want to. It's easier that way. It also enables them to look like knowledgeable insiders to their peers, bosses and (or so they think) their readers. But many readers think reporters use blind quotes from unidentified (and nonexistent) sources simply to give voice to their own views. Even if reputable reporters don't do that, they may attribute to an unidentified "source" a quote that synthesizes the views of several sources, no one of whom said precisely the words the reporter needed to make a particular point in his story. I think of that as the equivalent of a composite character. I also think of that by another name. Fiction.

Basically, the use of unnamed sources is a bad habit—a self-perpetuating phenomenon. Sources have come to expect anonymity because reporters grant it so willingly, so sources insist on it and reporters have to grant it and sources.... In the course of my twenty-three years as the *Los Angeles Times* media critic, I've frequently been interviewed by other reporters writing about the media—especially in recent years, when changes at the *Times* itself have often been big journalistic news—and I've been amazed by how many reporters will call and offer me anonymity before I've said a word. "We can do this off the record if you want," they'll say.

It's one thing to succumb to a source's demand for anonymity—grudgingly, after a passionate, well-reasoned argument; it's quite another to offer anonymity to a source before you've asked a single question or had even the slightest indication that he's uncomfortable speaking *on* the record. When I tell these reporters that I only speak on the record, they automatically assume that I won't say anything negative. "No," I assure them, "I'll be candid with you." I also tell them that I only speak on the record as a matter of self-preservation. When I started writing about the media, I knew that my *Times* colleagues would probably assume that as the in-house media maven, I was the likely source of any *Times* gossip that appeared elsewhere. So I adopted my only-on-the-record policy and told my *Times* colleagues, "If my name isn't on it, I didn't say it." I've since angered many of my colleagues, both by what I've written about them, their friends and our paper in our paper, as well as by what I've said in other publications. But at least they knew who said it and whom to complain to.

David Shaw is media critic for the Los Angeles Times *and a Pulitzer Prize winner. His most recent book is* The Pleasure Police.

3

Rushing to Judgment

Ann Compton

There are more cameras trained on the president of the United States than on any other living person on this earth. There are more eyes around the world ready to judge him. And the small band of us standing there as journalists have the job every single day of showing the world a fair picture of the man. It ought to be simple.

But in the steamy climate of character stories dominating White House coverage these days, fairness to the president, to all public figures, and even to private citizens is often ignored, especially under the pressure of deadlines and competition.

In the twenty-three years since I first walked up the White House driveway as an ABC News correspondent, no story has been easier to distort than the Whitewater investigation and all that the phrase has come to include. Stir up a script about "missing billing records," "discovered in the family quarters," subpoenas, grand juries, the first lady and White House confidants, and we have a damning soup of accusations.

All of us who report on television from the field write our own material. Our producers review every syllable, except for our live stand-ups. But fairness is much more than telling the facts. We must tell them in such a way that the big picture conforms to the facts as we believe them. I want a viewer to take what I have distilled into a 90-second story and come away with the same impression of the facts that I came to after hours, even days, of reporting.

Covering political news is so very subjective that I have found that only experience and seasoned judgment are my guardians of fairness. Each story brings its own facts and shadings, and each demands that I take the time to weigh whether this word or that shot of the president's reaction gives the viewer the true impression. It is never easy, and the learning experience never stops.

What has forced our hand on fairness in the last few years is the heat of competition and the rush to publish in ways television and print reporters have never been pushed before. Consider how the Monica Lewinsky story broke: *Newsweek* decided to hold its revealing story for a week, believing that was fair to a criminal prosecutor who was closing in on a key witness. *Newsweek* did the right thing. But someone at the magazine apparently disagreed. The woman's name and key details leaked into the Drudge Report, an Internet gossip page that does not seem bound by the same limits of fairness. Enter the political forces in Washington. On ABC News' "This Week," Republican commentator William Kristol deliberately dropped a mention of the *Newsweek* angle. News anchor Sam Donaldson, quite correctly, cut him off. But within days ABC News and other organizations were able to confirm within court circles the basic elements of the story: that prosecutor Kenneth Starr believed he had come across serious evidence the president may have suborned perjury of the witness and may have obstructed justice. Now, that was a fair peg on which to hang the real red meat— another woman who got too close to the president.

Newsweek, scooped on its own story, found two ways to catch up, neither inherently unfair. It used its Web site to publish exclusive details of the magazine's long investigation, and it dispatched its reporter and his senior editors to our television talk shows to take credit for *Newsweek*'s great find. That also allowed us to carry the story forward, using fellow reporters as our very public sources. Fair? Yes.

But that also unleashed frenzied days of competition in which fairness was forgotten. Two prestigious newspapers rushed sizzling details onto their Web sites, then had to recant. One was *The Dallas Morning News*, which later claimed its source did a complete 180-degree turnabout. The other was the venerable *Wall Street Journal*, taking back lurid details of a steward removing lipstick-stained tissues from the Oval Office. We refrained from reporting either Internet story, although later our own reporting found much of the information quite credible.

Early on, ABC News established a system by which a conference call was held every morning, seven days a week, and the team working the story connected information and fact checking through a constant stream of e-mail messages. But even that quality control was not enough. Details were then used by a widening circle of correspondents around the clock, from our "World News Now" broadcasts before dawn through

"Nightline" past midnight. Radio and ABCNews.com published around the clock.

As that circle expanded, the enforcement of fairness became more of a challenge. Correspondent Jackie Judd would write with painstaking care a two-minute story for the evening news, and then I would squeeze most of the information into a slightly shorter version for the next day's "Good Morning America." Radio's writers would combine our information with wire copy and fresh newspaper headlines and condense the facts into even smaller 30-second stories. The effect was often like that of a fun-house mirror—recognizable but distorted. Newswriters without firsthand knowledge from the sources could not be as exacting or subtle with the phrases they used. Eventually, the tabloid TV shows and newspapers went on to take a hard fact about the investigators' retrieval of a blue dress and make it into screaming headlines about lab testing of a semen-stained gown.

On any story, there are some tests of fairness that should be quite simple. One that has touched our White House coverage is a ban on candid cameras. The use of hidden cameras is unfair anytime the news subject has no idea at all that his or her actions are being recorded. Bill and Hillary Clinton complained they did not know news cameras were hiding in the weeds on their St. Thomas, V.I., vacation when they engaged in an impromptu fox-trot on a private beach. I'd agree—had the photographers actually been hiding. And ABC News strictly forbids the use of hidden cameras for daily hard-news coverage. But the private beach faced a very public ocean dotted with police and fishing boats. ABC News did have a camera on a chartered boat too far away to get such intimate video, but if I had a camera staked out with the others I would have used it. The Clintons were in full view of the neighbors and the Secret Service, and I find it impossible to believe they thought they were as out of sight as they would have been indoors.

My opinion runs the opposite way on a more narrow case with the Reagans years ago. At their remote mountaintop ranch in California, the only view of them mounting up their horses each morning was with an incredibly long lens from public parkland on the next ridge of mountains miles away. I said that went over the line into "peeping Tom journalism." ABC quit sending the expensive equipment out to cover Reagan vacation trips, although I fear, in the current climate, the long lenses would be common practice even for the networks these days, perhaps on the grounds the Reagans had to know cameras would be there.

Personally, I still believe truly hidden cameras have no role as tools in mainstream reporting—ever—even those that claim a noble purpose of exposing horrid conditions in nursing homes or child-care situations. It is one thing for television programs to air footage taped by parents in their own home of baby-sitters abusing children. But walking in the door to a repair shop or clinic or grocery claiming you are not a reporter is lying, plain and simple. I am not even comfortable with the policy at my own network where extraordinary approval from management is given on rare occasions for undercover surveillance carefully executed by some of our investigative programs. It makes better sense to me to find sources among legitimate employees or former workers. More difficult to document? Yes. More fair? Yes again.

In television, first impressions are the only impressions. Our television images carry tremendous power, and our words have instant impact that cannot be read over and over again like a newspaper's. As broadcasters, every day we have a special responsibility to make sure such impressions are fair. What kills us is time. Two minutes' time can be too little time in which to lay out our facts completely and fairly. Pushed by the clock we have no margin to go back and rewrite one more time.

Fairness is not in any user's manual handed to us with a White House press pass. Fairness is a principle, a way of working that we learn to apply to every story, every script, the choice of every sound bite and every stand-up close despite the rush to report in this era of competition.

Ann Compton is a White House correspondent for ABC News.

4

"Why Hurt Me?"

Walter Anderson

One morning in the early 1970s, when I was employed as an investigative reporter at Westchester Rockland Newspapers, an editor handed me a copy of *The New York Times* and pointed to a report of a cross that seemed to appear miraculously on the bathroom window of a tenement apartment in the South Bronx. We were in the heart of the Christmas season, only a few days before kids all over New York would be tearing open their presents.

"I don't believe this is anything but light on a window," the editor said, "but it's a helluva story. What could be better yarn than a miracle in so unlikely a place?"

When I reminded him that more than a few people believed a miracle had occurred in an even more unlikely place about twenty centuries ago, he told me, "Yeah, yeah. Good. Now go do the story."

This was a challenge. The *Times*, the *Daily News* and others had published thorough reports on the phenomenon, including community reaction. New York City television and radio stations, in a frenzy because of the timing, were all over the story. What could I do that would be different?

I noticed in all of the published and broadcast reports that the family members who lived in the apartment were reluctant to be interviewed in depth—which is, of course, the normal response from people unaccustomed to press attention. It was also clear to me that this family—a mother and her five children—was not attempting to proselytize or seek reward. They simply seemed to be nice people.

Could I get close enough to this family—closer than anyone had so far—to write a unique profile?

I had some things going for me. Because I had grown up in a tenement myself, I had a sure sense of the place and a pretty good idea of the kind of family I'd find. Also, I knew this particular neighborhood well because I had worked there only a short time before on a drug investigation. My greatest assets, though, were my ambition and my will to win—I wanted to beat everybody.

Two telephone calls to the family confirmed that they wanted no more attention. I was politely rejected.

I decided to make a visit without an invitation. I did so at night when, I suspected, I'd be the only reporter around—and I was.

After I located the apartment, I was able to persuade the family to invite me into their home. In retrospect, I think I know why I succeeded. The family was moved, if not astonished, that I had come to see them in the evening. And, more important, they heard something they liked in my voice: They knew I could be trusted.

Thus I enjoyed several hours of good conversation, coffee and lemon meringue pie. They showed me the cross on the glass. Whether it was an accident of light or something larger, I could not tell. The family's hospitality, though, was compelling. The mother even went out of her way to introduce me to her neighbors, one of whom confided that he too had witnessed an apparition in his window—an open book whose pages seemed to turn when cars drove along the street a few floors below. "Some say it's the Bible," he told me, "but I'm not saying that. I don't know what it is."

I was particularly taken with the mother, though, and decided I'd focus the story on her. Her courage transcended the vision on the glass.

She reminded me of some women I knew as a child. They were solid, no matter how daunting the storm. Like them, she was kind and as tough as she needed to be—which is to say resilient. Mainly, though, this woman was centered—*family* centered—and I admired her. In one of the most violent, high-crime, drug-dealing neighborhoods in the New York metropolitan area, her five children were making it, attending school, on their way.

I felt terrific, elevated.

Later that night, I returned to the city room and typed what I was sure was the story I was born to tell.

When the article appeared the following day, the kudos, as I had expected, came in bunches: notes and calls from fellow reporters and editors, even a compliment from the grouch who had assigned me the story. I accepted the praise gracefully. This was good, very good.

Then I made a telephone call to the family.

When the mother answered, I cheerily inquired, "So, how did you like the story?"

She did not like it.

"Terrible...terrible," she said, her voice muffled, as if she were speaking through a handkerchief.

"I don't understand!" I blurted. "What are you talking about?"

Because she was sobbing, her reply was barely comprehensible, and I had to strain to understand. "Terrible..." she said, "and I trusted you.... Why hurt me? What did I do to *you*?"

Her voice was cracking, her words breaking through tears. This was real sorrow. It was deep hurt, not anger. I was flabbergasted, and her pain cut into me. I felt fear—a selfish fear that I had made a mistake that would cause me embarrassment or get me into trouble. Then I felt profound guilt that my first concern had been for me and not for this decent human being, whom I had somehow damaged.

"What do you mean?" I asked. "I don't understand. What did I do?"

There was another muffled response. I could hear the telephone drop.

One of her sons, a young teen-ager, picked up the phone and asked, "Mr. Anderson?"

"Yes!" I said. "What did I do?"

"You don't know?"

"No!" I insisted.

"That line in your story..." he said, his voice angry. "You told everybody that my mother was an unmarried mother of five. *Unmarried*! My mother trusted you! Why did you write that? Why is that anybody's business? You had no right to do this to my mother." And he hung up the telephone.

Over time, I would write other newspaper and magazine articles and books, become editor of a newspaper and, eventually, editor of a popular magazine. But it was then, in that moment, that I first began to value the concept of "fairness" in reporting. An innocent, courageous woman had paid a price for me.

I suppose it could be said that fairness is treating everybody in the same way, regardless of our own feelings or interests. That would imply that we should recognize our own biases for or against a subject. OK. In the story I've told, my bias was in *favor* of this mother of five. Moreover, not only was I predisposed to like her, I identified with her. Yet, unintentionally, I had hurt her.

The article I wrote was accurate, but I don't think it was fair. I had gotten the facts right, but *I* was not right.

I remember clearly agonizing over that disturbing telephone call and finally asking myself: If I had not used the adjective "unmarried," would the story have been incomplete or diminished? Was it necessary to understanding the story?

No.

The boy's question, I recognized, was defining: "Why is that anybody's business?"

It was, I realized too late, nobody's business. And I was also acutely aware that I could not ease the embarrassment I had caused.

So, when the topic of "fairness" emerged years later in a meeting at the Media Studies Center, I told the story I've recounted here and said that, if I could choose whether I'd be known as honest, fair or accurate, I'd like to be known as fair. I also want to be honest and accurate, of course, but mainly I want to be fair.

I've reinforced to many editors over the last quarter of a century the insight that editing solely to avoid a potential libel suit is not a measure of fairness but a measure of prudence. A story may be free of libel yet still be unfair.

But what is real fairness?

I remember some advice I heard that mother in the South Bronx give her children: "Treat each other with respect."

Each other, I've learned, means *everybody*, not merely those of us who are lucky enough to be paid to communicate.

We have the freedom to report facts and the responsibility to choose what facts to report.

The question is, What will we *choose* to do?

Walter Anderson is editor in chief of Parade *magazine.*

5

My Failure to Be Fair to the President

Nat Hentoff

Milt Hinton, a revered bass player whose career has encompassed much of jazz history, tells younger musicians: "Unless you've had experience and lived, what could you have to say on your instrument?" And with experience come enthusiasm, prejudices and pronounced opinions.

As Randall Kennedy emphasized in his essay on the Supreme Court in the winter, 1998 *Media Studies Journal*: "[T]here is no such thing as an unbiased observer. To recognize and concede one's own ideological proclivities need not prevent a journalist from offering accurate reportage and insightful analysis. Indeed, the reverse is more likely: The reporter who is more self-conscious and open about his or her ideological leanings is more likely to be a more sophisticated and credible analyst."

And more likely to be a reporter whose work is fair.

Even at my beginning in journalism fifty years ago, I began to recognize that objectivity—though prized by a good many editors then— was illusory. Nevertheless, by remaining aware of my biases and fencing them off from my reporting, I learned I could be closer to being fair. Fairness means you get the facts, all of them that you can, especially when they surprise you into re-evaluating what you thought the story was going to be about when you began.

It doesn't always work. I was doing a story on a Southern Baptist preacher a few years ago, and when I first saw him with his long black coat and piercing gaze, I figured this guy was hardly a civil libertarian. But then he spoke, and he sounded like William O. Douglas and William Brennan. The preacher was opposed, for example, to all forms of censorship because the framers of the Constitution, he said, intended Americans to think for themselves.

Later, ashamed, I told him how I had prejudged him. "Well," he said, "there is a censorship of stereotype, of caricature. You know that someone is a Baptist minister, so you already know what he's going to say before he says it. So you shut him off."

Most of the time, however, I'm able to distance myself from my preconceptions, and when I'm slipping, I see the Baptist minister before me.

Fairness is not the only reason to be fair. A journalist survives on the basis of credibility, of integrity. A letter to the editor that exposes you for committing serious errors in your story can come back and haunt you a long time after. Many journalists have very thin skin. Also, many of us make enemies because of what we write, and they keep dossiers.

Accuracy, along with fairness, also helps a lot to counter libel suits. I was once sued by a school board for writing of appalling cases of corporal punishment in the city's schools. But I had affidavits from parents and X-rays of some of the kids' injuries. The suit was dropped.

There are times, however, when the person being written about makes it very difficult to see beneath his or her repellent qualities. I have followed Louis Farrakhan's career from when he was a protégé of Malcolm X—whose death he later called for—in the Nation of Islam. I am Jewish and I grew up in a city, Boston, that was virulently anti-Semitic, due in large part to Father Charles Coughlin—the radio priest of the 1930s whose broadcasts were laced with anti-Semitism. I also knew the work and impact of Gerald L.K. Smith and other dangerous anti-Semites. Since Farrakhan is the pre-eminent American anti-Semite these days, I write about him with a powerful bias.

But I dutifully hear his speeches, read his interviews, talk to people who know him and still find nothing to be fair about.

While I don't feel guilty about my reporting on Farrakhan, I am somewhat uneasy about the many columns and articles I've written about Bill Clinton. I fantasize about meeting him and having him ask, "Have you written anything, a single piece about me, that's favorable?"

After a long, uncomfortable pause, I would have to say, "No."

The anger about Clinton that drives my writing has nothing to do with his sexual trysts or even about the corruption among a good many of his cabinet members whom he, after all, appointed. My "special interest" as a journalist and citizen (there is no separating the two) is the Constitution. And no president in American history has done more diversified damage to the Constitution than Clinton. It is a profound failure of the American press that there has hardly been any reporting on this, except for Anthony Lewis of *The New York Times* and a very few other journalists. And when the press, out of indifference or ignorance, does not write about what is happening to the Constitution under Clinton, it too is as culpable as the president for the reduction of our liberties.

The oldest basic right in the English-speaking world is *habeas corpus*—the right to petition a federal court to review the actual fairness (due process) of a trial or of a sentence in state court. Included are death sentences.

Because of Clinton's leadership, Congress has reduced the right to petition for a writ of *habeas corpus* to one year. I have in my files, as do other reporters, records of men on death row who have finally been released after six to eight to 10 years—through *habeas corpus*—when their innocence has finally been proven through DNA or other means. But now, due to Clinton's evisceration of *habeas corpus*, some of the prisoners now condemned to death—some of whom, if history is any guide, are actually innocent—will be executed.

Clinton's contempt for First Amendment rights was shown when he pushed his Justice Department to urgently defend the Communications Decency Act, which would have essentially prohibited anything on the Internet that is not suitable for children. The Supreme Court disagreed with him, 9 to 0.

A basic rule in our system of law is that you can't be punished without first seeing—and being able to rebut—the evidence against you. Yet Clinton pushed successfully for an anti-terrorism law permitting the deportation of aliens suspected of "terrorism"—without allowing the aliens, or their lawyers, to know the evidence against them.

Robyn Blumner, an expert on civil liberties and a columnist for the *St. Petersburg* (Fla.) *Times*, notes: "One would be hard-pressed to find a constitutional right that Clinton has not attacked legislatively or in the courts." For example, she adds, "he has signed into law legislation that stripped the courts of jurisdiction to hear claims of rights violations by the government against immigrants and prisoners—both marginal populations with virtually no political power."

And Clinton has tried to do more to weaken the Constitution. He has advocated warrantless police searches of public housing apartments, and he has supported the use of roving FBI wiretaps so that a warrant for a wiretap on one phone would be extended to every other phone—without additional warrants—used by the person under suspicion.

Focusing on Clinton's attacks on our basic guarantees of rights and liberties, I have not written favorably about anything else Clinton has done. My disgust at his rampant violations of the Constitution, very much including the Bill of Rights, has thoroughly undermined my commitment to fairness.

Yet I am in favor of his efforts to provide uninsured children with health insurance, his proposal to limit class size in public schools and his plan to insure funds to provide students with mentors. Being able to know and to learn from adults with experience in the world can be very valuable for kids.

I can't deny that I should have written about some of Clinton's useful and innovative ideas, and maybe, prodded by having to write this article, I will. Maybe.

Nat Hentoff, a staff writer for the Village Voice *and a syndicated columnist for The* Washington Post, *is author or editor of more than 25 books, including his memoir,* Speaking Freely.

6

Shattering the Prism of Our Own Prejudice

Fergal Keane

The telephone rang and out of the fog of sleep I reached over and picked it up. "You won't believe this," said the voice of my assistant. He sounded genuinely excited. "It's really big news. Have you got a pen ready?" My heart began to race. He would never dream of calling me at 6 o'clock in the morning without good reason. I was a BBC correspondent and this assistant—whose name I will spare—was my eyes and ears in South Africa's tangled and troubled world of black township politics. He was plugged into the main black organizations in a way that no white reporter could ever hope to be.

"Buthelezi is stepping down as chief minister of KwaZulu. It looks like he's getting out of politics altogether," said my friend. He was referring to Chief Mangosuthu Buthelezi, leader of the predominantly Zulu Inkatha Freedom Party and the main black opponent of Nelson Mandela and his African National Congress. For years supporters of the two men had been engaged in bloody battles in South Africa's townships and in the hills of Natal Province. Of late the violence looked as if it might lead to full-scale civil war. Thus my assistant's news was staggering.

"Why is he going?" I asked. My friend replied that nobody seemed to know just yet. I pressed him on his sources. "It's been officially announced. I've checked it. It's true," he said. I put the phone down and immediately rang the news desk in London. "Buthelezi is quitting as chief minister of Natal." I said. "I'll be back with a dispatch as soon as possible." It was still very early in the morning in London, and the main bulletins were not due for another hour or so. Still, the news of Chief Buthelezi's resignation did make it onto one show.

I had only just replaced the receiver after talking to London when the telephone rang again. It was my assistant and he was laughing. "What's so funny?" I asked, my voice thickening with concern. "April Fool, April Fool," he chuckled down the line. "Buthelezi isn't stepping down." My knees began to wobble and I felt a surge of nausea. This was the least funny thing to happen to me in many long years. My friend sensed my concern. "It was just a joke," he offered. I exploded. "How could you? What kind of idiot are you? I trusted you and went to air with that story."

I told him to call me back and then I telephoned London. Happily the story had been broadcast only once on a minor radio backwater. I was able to kill it off before the main bulletins went on the air. "Somebody played a trick on me," I said weakly as the news editor began his interrogation. He pointed out—quite correctly—that as the person who had called in with the story, I was the one ultimately responsible. "The buck stops with you," he barked. "Thank heavens we managed to kill it in time."

I spent most of the day in a state of advanced rage. Naturally enough I directed most of the hostility toward my assistant. But I was also angry with myself, for I had breached one of the most sacred tenants of the journalistic trade: Always check the story yourself. No matter how much I trusted my assistant or how much I regarded his contacts and expertise, I should have checked the story out myself. After more than 15 years in journalism, after covering numerous conflicts and with long experience of South Africa, I still managed to make one of the most basic mistakes of all. Although I was profoundly shaken and humbled by the experience at the time, it took the passage of years for me to be able to examine its significance.

Yes, of course, there was a basic journalistic lesson to be learned—that was self-evidently clear. But I had to ask myself whether there was not a deeper truth to be rooted out and considered. To do this I had to cast my mind back to those frequently terrible days of the early 1990s when the township wars were claiming hundreds of lives.

Much of my working life was spent covering the vicious conflict between Buthelezi's Inkatha and Mandela's ANC, which seemed set to derail the transition to a nonracial democracy. Buthelezi's threats to set up an independent Zulu state threatened to lead to a full-scale civil war. He had allied himself with right-wing groups and had walked out of the country's multiparty talks. To his own Zulu supporters and to conservative whites, Buthelezi was a hero, a man who stood up to the ANC and the National Party of President F.W. De Klerk. But to a majority in the country he was a reactionary figure, one who threatened to ignite terrible conflict.

Buthelezi's relations with the press were deplorably bad. At news conferences he became hostile with even the most gently probing questioner and frequently turned on those journalists he regarded as impertinent or anti-Inkatha. The majority of the foreign and domestic press loathed Buthelezi and saw him as a spoiler, a man who had decided to go to war because he feared his own power would be diminished in a South Africa run by Mandela and the ANC.

In my BBC reporting and in a subsequent book on South Africa, I went out of my way to try and see things from Buthelezi's point of view. This was my conscious mind at work. My BBC training taught me that fairness was an absolute. It was not something to compromise. But the reality is that I was as much prone to the prevailing mood in the foreign press as anybody else. I wanted South Africa to be a free, peaceful and democratic country, and there was a great deal about Buthelezi's behavior to suggest that he wasn't going to allow this to happen. And so when I received that early morning phone call from a trusted aide telling me that Buthelezi was stepping down was I—in my heart of hearts—not secretly relieved and pleased? The answer is very probably YES. I thought this would save a great deal of conflict and make a settlement much easier. Peace would be that much clearer.

I cannot say that this alone made me run with the story. I would never run with a story simply because I wanted it to be true. In simple journalistic terms it was a good tale, the kind of story you want to be first with. But with the wisdom of hindsight, I also know that my deeper feelings about Buthelezi played a part. Perhaps, I thought to myself, there would be fewer massacres to cover, fewer mass funerals and a general reduction in the level of tension we all lived with in those strange times.

Buthelezi, of course, did not step down. He stayed on, took part in the elections at the last moment and then became a minister under Mandela in South Africa's first nonracial government.

As for me, I left South Africa and Buthelezi behind after the elections. But I believe the "April Fool" call did change me as a journalist. It taught me that when I am dealing with characters or organizations toward whom I have any negative feelings, I must insert an extra caution.

In a journalistic world crowded with demon figures—Bosnian Serbs and Rwandan Hutus, to name but two—I believe it is essential to deeply question our reporting. It is perfectly legitimate to have personal feelings. But we must be rigorous in ensuring that they do not consciously or—as can happen frequently—subconsciously affect our handling of stories.

This is particularly difficult when the subject is a person or group with a proven track record of violence or disagreeable behavior. The fact that Hutu extremists committed one of the most horrific crimes of the 20th century—the 1994 genocide of the Tutsis—does not mean that we can accept each and every story we hear about their activities. Their leaders may be among the most loathsome people in the history of the century, but that does not imply that I can run with stories about them or their activities for which there is simply no proof.

I would go further and say that hate figures demand of us an extra sensitivity, a greater commitment to fairness. One may well ultimately reach the same conclusion as the partisan reporter, but at least it will be based on knowledge and inquiry. We must be especially wary of the media consensus—the general climate in which one group is seen as totally bad and the other is proclaimed good.

This may seem like a terribly basic and self-evident comment. But I am increasingly struck by the reluctance of journalists to question their own motives. Too many in our ranks are infected with the self-importance and spurious notions of moral superiority. We demand from others that they be open and accountable and yet erect stockades when asked to discuss our own mistakes.

I know that when I was asked to write this article and to reflect on a past journalistic mistake, I felt distinctly uneasy. Nobody likes to admit he got something wrong. And yet such disclosure is the lifeblood of healthy journalism. Arrogance, self-importance and defensiveness induce a journalistic myopia. We end up seeing the world through the prism of our own prejudice.

Because so much of what we do is quickly produced and just as quickly forgotten, it is easy to believe that there are no durable lessons to be learned from our work. My Buthelezi story lasted only a few seconds on the early morning airwaves and was killed off before any damage was done. But I know that I learned a vital lesson from the experience: I must take nothing for granted, least of all my own journalism.

Fergal Keane has covered international crises in Northern Ireland, southern Africa and Asia as a BBC correspondent. His reporting on Rwanda earned him the Overseas Press Club's Edward R. Murrow award. He is the author of Season of Blood.

7

Giving People What They Deserve

Joann Byrd

I'm pretty sure it was a few days after the 1984 presidential election. I know it was a time when my newspaper, *The Herald* in Everett, Wash., and every other newspaper in the United States was reporting the election. A postcard arrived in *The Herald* executive editor's in-box, and it asked a question that made me squirm: "Why don't you publish the number of votes cast for Socialist Party candidates, or for any candidates other than the Republicans and Democrats?"

I believe my correspondent was a Mrs. Wright, and I bet she would be happy to know she started something. Worrying and nagging, mostly. And making me think that the rest of the editors in the country ought to be squirming too.

The reason Mrs. Wright's question resonated so was that I was a stickler for fairness. I didn't follow a former boss's technique of measuring lines of type to be certain that candidates were getting equity, but I had been known to preach that both candidates in each race were to be given something close to even attention. Fairness, I always figured, was one thing readers and candidates and people on both sides of every issue ought to get from the newspaper. So, why didn't we report the vote tallies for the candidates of parties other than the Democrats and Republicans?

I couldn't tell Mrs. Wright that no one would care about the Socialist candidates' votes, because at the minimum, the people who voted for the Socialists (probably including Mrs. Wright) would care. And even voters who regularly choose the Democrat or the Republican might be curious about their competition.

I couldn't say it didn't matter because the Socialists were so far away from becoming the winners that a Socialist couldn't win if every single absentee was for the Socialists. We already knew that. And that wasn't the point.

After thinking it over, it became obvious to me that the fairness I was so fond of extended only to those who won or came in second. I had never even entertained the possibility of covering minor-party candidates, either during the campaign or in the election results. Oh, we covered the antics of the occasional novelty candidate who was having fun on the ballot. But the others, who actually wanted to be elected, and who had ideas about the tax structure and foreign affairs and social change? We never thought of them as true contenders. At *The Herald*, where we tried to use our precious space for news that mattered, the Democrats and the Republicans were just about the whole story.

I phoned Mrs. Wright and said I thought she had raised an interesting point, and that I was going to think about it. Something was indeed wrong if the press—in theory the champion of independent thinking, free speech and the underdog—was routinely dismissing candidates who embodied those characteristics.

In the next few elections, *The Herald* printed some additional vote tallies even though I remember AP had to make some special effort to get them for us.

The error of the media's ways was made even more clear by a piece by Howard Kurtz, *The Washington Post* media critic, which bore the headline "In Quadrennial Rite, Press Bestows Front-Runner Status: It's Clinton." The story ran in the *Post* on Jan. 12, 1992.

I was then getting ready to head to the *Post* as the paper's ombudsman. Kurtz's report pointed out a feature of modern campaigns that exacerbates our fundamental unfairness. Not only do the news media cover only the likely winners, we pick them out in the first place. The media have taken over the major parties' role in choosing the candidates who will get the money and the attention—and therefore, in all likelihood, the votes. We do this, as Larry Sabato, a University of Virginia political scientist, said to Kurtz, by covering politics as "a game that has someone who's winning and someone who's losing. This is a nonideological way of sorting out the process."

Sabato's insight was to notice the "nonideological" nature of the media's collective thinking. We christen the front-runner not saying he *should* win, but that he *will* win. That fact—or at least that he will come close—is what triggers our traditional news judgment: The people likely to govern the country (or the state or the city or the water district) are the ones most important for people to know about.

It's much simpler for us—and for readers and viewers, probably—
to keep track of only two candidates. Most newsrooms don't have enough
people to report the campaigns of everyone who runs for president.
And most newsrooms also have races for city hall, the state house and
the water commission to attend to. And if readers and viewers didn't
know Sophie Socialist was running, then what sense would it make to
report the votes she got?

In my three years at the *Post*, representatives of minor parties called
to complain that their candidates weren't getting a fair shake from any
of the media. Other candidates wanted to know how they were supposed to get their ideas to the populace if the media ignored them. By
then, I was converted.

I nagged. Especially I nagged the *Post*. The editor of another big
newspaper read one of my columns on this subject and phoned to say I
had made him feel guilty. In fact, guilt and contemplation were the
primary results of my sermons. There was talk at the *Post* and, I'm
told, elsewhere. But I've seen no change in the way the *Post* or any
other news medium treats candidates of minor parties.

Actually, that is not surprising. This is a battle against news judgment, news judgment that has been working for us for a very long time
and that traditionally works best without conditions and exceptions.
Though we try to use an even hand covering competing sides of an
issue and the opponents in an election, news judgment isn't about equity. The skier who won the men's downhill gets the attention. The
woman who becomes CEO is profiled on the business-section front.
The woman who contributes most to the community gets the longest
obituary. News judgment is a fair system because it depends on what
the story subjects do: Getting ahead and staying ahead keeps that candidate in the news. If thousands of people show up at every campaign
event, there's reason for us to be covering that candidate.

But what makes it unfair to leave news judgment on autopilot in
campaigns is that we have so much influence over who gets out front
at the start. The media do not, and should not, work for the candidates. The fact that money and support flow to the people we declare
likely to succeed is an unintended consequence of our reporting reality (though it's a consequence we know about and should acknowledge in our thinking).

But we do work for voters, and through them, for the collective
community. Denying a candidate coverage could, at least theoreti-
cally, deny voters a great leader. It certainly denies voters a demo-

cratic process based on a full-service marketplace of ideas and a fully informed public.

Fairness is giving people what they deserve. Whether it's candidates or communities who are badly served by this habit of ours, they all deserve more from us.

I've had a multitude of elections to crystallize my thinking since Mrs. Wright wrote me. And I am certain of one thing: If we are anointing the front-runners in January, fairness to our readers and viewers and their candidates requires that we cover, before and after the election, the people who don't get that nod.

Joann Byrd, a 1989–90 Media Studies Center fellow, is editorial page editor of The Seattle Post-Intelligencer. *She was ombudsman of the* Washington Post *and executive editor of* The Herald *(Everett, Wash.).*

8

An Embattled Foreign Correspondent

Suzanne Levy

I hope that the American people are grateful for what I did. For five years, on a regular basis, I fought the more extreme attempts by my editors at the BBC back in Britain to portray America as a land full of gun-toting, bible-bashing, collagen-filled lunatics. (A losing battle perhaps, but more later.)

I naively wanted my reporting to reflect in some small way the normalcy of everyday life I saw around me while living in the States. Motivated by some idea of fairness, I thought I should offer what I thought was reality. Wrong! What my editors wanted was facelifts for dogs in Beverly Hills, and they wanted them now.

In essence, they sought to have their (oh so British) prejudices about Yanks confirmed. These were 1990s prejudices, mind you, newly minted. (Previous stereotypes had included the 1970s rich, plaid-trouser-wearing American tourists pointing at Buckingham Palace and pronouncing it "quaint.") Now the stereotypes were far less benign. They wanted Wacko Jacko and his oxygen tent, they wanted A Life Of Fear in the Bronx, they wanted pet cemeteries in space—anything that would give the listener or viewer a chance to shake her head in incredulity and feel smug about British common sense and moderation.

Believe me, I tried to be fair, but in the end it was hard to resist this siren call. I knew that one wacky story was surrounded by a thousand normal ones, but somehow the journalist in me kidnapped my sense of fair play. There were truly too many bizarre stories to be reported. Americans simply did not help me in my desire to convey the country as a haven of day-to-day mundane living. So I wrestled with my conscience—and America lost.

For example, the British public is now fully aware of the phenomenon of pectoral implants for men—yes, now even the scrawniest man on the beach in Venice, Calif., can have a chest like Arnold Schwarzenegger. Pop in a silicon bag and away you go. The fact that this was limited to a handful of vain males in California was neither here nor there. I tracked down a plastic surgeon in Los Angeles who confessed to performing such operations and found a bodybuilder who confessed to cheating in competitions. Perfect.

Or the Erotic Bakery in New York City. Cakes made in all anatomically correct shapes and sizes. (Use your imagination.) When asked exactly how correct, the shop owner looked me straight in the eye and said, "Well, we've got circumcised ones over there." That was it. Straight into the British tabloids before you could say "hold the marzipan."

Or the Santa Barbarans who, in a drought, were distraught over their dried out brown lawns. They missed the emerald perfection—so they did the most obvious thing. They dyed them. Lawn after lawn sprayed a gorgeous green. A well-received report and another stereotype fulfilled: appearance over everything. (Read: those Yanks are just so superficial.)

Do I feel guilty? Of course. I could have reported about the fiscal deficit. Instead I wrote about America's oddities, and the British went to bed safe in their knowledge that their Atlantic neighbors were completely mad.

There were times when I drew a line, however. The stories I've mentioned were ultimately harmless fun, despite a creeping accumulative effect. But when I was phoned and asked to cover a story about "kids in the Bronx wearing bulletproof vests to school" that had been printed in a tabloid, it was time to reflect. If I did the story (and I was not convinced it was even true), then the British public would think that American schools were completely out of control—the Wild West gone mad. I knew that while there were pockets of violence, and some reports of kids being shot in school, these were the exception, a tiny minority. If I did a report on this latest phenomenon, it would promote an image that was fundamentally false. This one school would come to represent *all* the schools in America from Des Moines to Detroit. I thought it over, phoned my editors and squashed the story.

But if I thought I was guilty of unfair representation of a foreign culture, I am afraid to say that the American portrayal of British life beat me hands down. I was astonished to see what few stories made it into the main network news—and then appalled to see their subjects. In fact I hesitate to say "subjects" because they barely made it into the plural. There were two subjects only—the Royals and the Eccentrics.

Diana's death may have given a soberness to the reporting, but a few years ago royal fever was in full swing. Reported like an episode of "Dynasty," the coverage was comparable to that in the United Kingdom but with deference replaced by fairy-tale awe. As far as I could see, the British Royals were covered as if they were Disney kings and queens, with little sense of their place in British politics or any coverage of the debate about their role in society.

The British upper crust also seem to crop up regularly in American advertising. A Little Lord Fauntleroy type was used to sell Fig Newtons, I seem to remember ("It's not a cookie, Mother, it's a Fig Newton"), and a butler sold Maxell cassette tapes. What I never saw were any middle-class accents or, heaven forbid, cockney or any regional accents. It was as if Britain were only interesting if it stayed in the 19th century, in arrested development, somewhere between Dickens and "Upstairs Downstairs."

Almost as a tit-for-tat for my coverage of strange new Californian trends, the American correspondents in the U.K. had obviously been briefed by *their* editors to go on a search for that lovable strand of British society known as the Eccentric. I once watched a story on an American network about a Scottish laird in some remote part of the Highlands who was so crazy that his closest companions were his sheep. Oddly I can't quite remember the details. I can only imagine the reporter traveled three days and three nights to find such a man, and I hope he was well rewarded for his troubles.

The stereotype here, of course, is that Britain is full of nonconformists who refuse to act sensibly like Americans and instead value individual behavior over the well-being of the group. Which translates in the American imagination into a wild-haired 60-year-old fierce Englishwoman who drives alone across the Sahara in a Landrover for a "bit of fun."

Does this unbalanced coverage ultimately matter? Probably not. It would be impossible for any foreign reporter to accurately portray life as he or she found it—there's simply not the time on the airwaves or the column inches. And the news agenda, dominated by politics in Westminster and Washington, will always keep a reporter on the straight and narrow. But we can affect the way people think of a foreign society, and so we should consider what is fair—and what is not.

Ironically, I found this out in my own life just after I'd arrived in New York and was being interviewed to share an apartment by a woman

I'd just met. After some general questions, she turned and asked whether I drank tea at 3 o'clock every day. When I demurred, incredulously, and told her that I drank coffee, not tea, the woman told me how disappointed she was—she was so hoping my British habits would rub off on her.

I do hope she wasn't referring to the sheep-loving Scottish laird.

Suzanne Levy, a 1992–93 Media Studies Center fellow, is a producer/director for BBC Television and Radio.

Part 2

Fairness—A History

9

In All Fairness

Michael Schudson

Everybody's a media critic in a democracy. The news media are the chief institutions for making our public life visible, and a lot rides on how they present us to ourselves. As citizens, we have a stake in trying to make our standards theirs. So people complain that the news media are too liberal—or too conservative. The media overplay violence—or they sanitize it. They are the lapdogs of their corporate owners—or they bite the economic system that feeds them. They are insufferably prurient—or they are rigidly puritanical. They are insidiously partisan—or they are boringly neutral. And on and on. Where have you been, Monica Lewinsky?

American journalists, buffeted by critics from every corner and wracked by self-criticism too, have long insisted that they try to be fair. But what's fair? That has changed from one era to the next.

In colonial journalism, printers proclaimed their concern for fairness in order to shed responsibility for what appeared in their pages. Benjamin Franklin insisted in his "Apology for Printers," published in 1731, that the printer was just that—one who prints, not one who edits, exercises judgment or agrees with each opinion in his pages. "Printers are educated in the Belief that when Men differ in Opinion, both Sides ought equally to have the Advantage of being heard by the Publick; and that when Truth and Error have fair Play, the former is always an over-match for the latter: Hence they chearfully serve all contending Writers that pay them well, without regarding on which side they are of the Question in Dispute."

At first, colonial printers did not imagine their newspapers to be either political instruments or professional agencies of news gathering.

39

None of the early papers reached out to collect news; they printed what came to them. Colonial printers, more than their London brethren, were public figures—running the post office, serving as clerks for the government and printing the laws. But they were also small businessmen who were careful not to offend their customers.

In the first half-century of American journalism, little indicated that the newspaper would become a central forum for political discourse. Colonial printers avoided controversy when they could, preached the printer's neutrality when they had to and printed primarily foreign news because it afforded local readers and local authorities no grounds for grumbling. Out of a sample of 1,900 items Franklin's weekly *Pennsylvania Gazette* printed from 1728 to 1765, only 34 touched on politics in Philadelphia or Pennsylvania.

As conflict with England heated up after 1765, politics entered the press and printerly "fairness" went by the board. In a time when nearly everyone felt compelled to take sides, printers found neutrality harder to maintain than partisanship. The newspaper began its long career as the mouthpiece of political parties and factions. Patriots had no tolerance for the pro-British press, and the new states passed and enforced treason and sedition statutes.

American victory in the war for independence did not bring immediate freedom for the press. During the state-by-state debates over ratification of the Constitution in 1787 and 1788, Federalists dominated the press and squeezed Antifederalists out of public debate. In Pennsylvania, leading papers tended not to report Antifederalist speeches at the ratification convention. When unusual newspapers in Philadelphia, New York and Boston sought to report views on both sides, Federalists stopped their subscriptions and forced the papers to end their attempt at evenhandedness.

Some of the nation's founders supported outspoken political criticism so long as they were fighting a monarchy for their independence but held that open critique of a duly elected republican government could be legitimately curtailed. Sam Adams, the famed Boston agitator during the struggle for independence, changed his views on political action once republican government was established. This great advocate of open talk, committees of correspondence, an outspoken press and voluntary associations of citizens now opposed all hint of public associations and public criticism that operated outside the regular channels of government. As one contemporary of Adams observed, it did no harm for writers to mislead the people when the people were powerless, but "To mislead the judgement of the people, where they have all power, must produce the greatest possible mischief."

The Sedition Act of 1798 forbade criticism of the Federalist government and as many as one in four editors of oppositional papers were brought up on charges under this law. But this went one step further than many Americans of the day could stomach. Federalist propaganda notwithstanding, Thomas Jefferson won the presidency in 1800. The Sedition Act expired, party opposition began to be grudgingly accepted and a more libertarian theory of the press gained ground.

In 19th-century journalism, editors came to take great pride in the speed and accuracy of the news they provided. With the introduction in the 1830s of the rotary press and soon the steam-powered press, amidst an expanding urban economy on the Eastern seaboard and the rush of enthusiasm for Jacksonian democracy, commercial competition heated up among city newspapers. A new breed of "penny papers" hired newsboys to hawk copies on the street; penny-press editors competed for wider readership and increasingly sought out local news—of politics, crime and high society.

While this newly aggressive commercialism in journalism was an important precondition for modern notions of objectivity, at first it fostered only a narrow concept of stenographic fairness. Newspapers boasted more and more about the speed and accuracy of their news gathering, but editors found this perfectly consistent with political partisanship and choosing to cover only the speeches or rallies of their favorite party. It was equally consistent, in their eyes, for reporters to go over speeches with sympathetic politicians they had covered to improve, in printed form, on the oral presentation. Into the 1870s and 1880s, Washington correspondents routinely supplemented their newspaper income by clerking for the very congressional committees they wrote about.

As late as the 1890s, when a standard Republican paper covered a presidential election, it not only deplored and derided Democratic candidates in editorials but often neglected to mention them in the news. In the days before public-opinion polling, the size of partisan rallies was taken as a proxy for likely electoral results. Republican rallies would be described as "monster meetings" while Democratic rallies were often not covered at all. In the Democratic papers, of course, it was just the reverse.

While partisanship endured, reporters came to enjoy a culture of their own independent of political parties. They developed their own mythologies (reveling in their intimacy with the urban underworld), their own clubs and watering holes and their own professional practices. Interviewing, for instance, became a common activity for reporters only in the 1870s and 1880s. No president submitted to an interview before Andrew Johnson in 1868, but by the 1880s the interview was a well-accepted and institutionalized "media event," an occasion created by journalists from which they could then craft a story. This new journalistic practice did not erase partisanship. It did, however, foreshadow reporters' emerging dedication to a sense of craft. Journalists began to locate themselves in a new occupational culture with its own rules, its own rewards and its own *esprit*.

Interviewing was a practice oriented more to pleasing an audience of news consumers than to parroting or promoting a party line. By the 1880s, newspapers had become big business. They erected towering downtown buildings, employed scores of reporters, sponsored splashy civic festivals and ran pages of advertising from the newly burgeoning department stores. The papers vastly expanded their readership in this growing marketplace. Accordingly, reporters writing news came to focus less on promoting parties and more on making stories.

Yet not until the 1920s was American journalism characterized by what we might call modern analytical and procedural fairness. Analytical fairness had no secure place until journalists as an occupational group developed loyalties more to their audiences and to themselves as an occupational community than to their publishers or their publishers' favored political parties. At this point journalists also came to articulate rules of the journalistic road more often and more consistently. As an Associated Press executive declared in 1925, "If you do not remember anything else that I have said, I beg of you to remember this, for it is fundamental: The Associated Press never comments on the news."

This newly articulated fairness doctrine was related to the sheer growth in news gathering: Rules of objectivity enabled editors to keep lowly reporters in check, although they had less control over high-flying foreign correspondents. Objectivity as ideology was a kind of industrial discipline. At the same time, it seemed a natural and progressive ideology for an aspiring occupational group at a moment when science was god, efficiency was cherished, and increasingly prominent elites judged partisanship a vestige of the tribal 19th century. First Mugwump reformers, led by the Anglo-Saxon patricians of the Northeast during the late 19th century, and then the Progressives, who pursued a broader reform movement in the early 20th century, argued that politics itself should be beyond partisanship. No wonder journalists picked up on their appeal.

Yet at the very moment that journalists embraced "objectivity," they also recognized its limits. In the 1930s, there was a vogue for what contemporaries called "interpretive journalism." Leading journalists and journalism educators insisted that the world had grown increasingly complex and needed not only to be reported but explained. Political columnists, like Walter Lippmann, David Lawrence, Frank Kent and Mark Sullivan, came into their own. Journalists insisted that their task was to help readers not only to know but to understand. At the same time, they now took it for granted that understanding had nothing to do with party or partisan sentiment.

Was this progress? Was a professional press taking over from party hacks? Not everyone was sure. If the change brought a new dispassionate tone to news coverage, it also opened the way to making entertainment rather than political coherence a chief criterion of journalism.

Speaker of the House "Uncle" Joe Cannon objected in 1927: "I believe we had better publicity when the party press was the rule and the so-called independent press the exception, than we have now," he said in his autobiography, *Uncle Joe Cannon*. "The correspondents in the press gallery then felt their responsibility for reporting the proceedings of Congress. Then men representing papers in sympathy with the party in power were alert to present the record their party was making so that the people would know its accomplishments, and those representing the opposition party were eager to expose any failures on the part of the Administration." In the independent press, in contrast, serious discussion of legislation gave way to entertainment: "The cut of a Congressman's whiskers or his clothes is a better subject for a human interest story than what he says in debate."

News, Cannon mourned, had replaced legislative publicity. What had really happened was that journalists had become their own interpretive community, writing to one another and not to parties or partisans.

The triumph of an ethic of analytical and procedural fairness (or "objectivity" as it has presumptuously been called) was never complete. Even journalism's leaders took it for granted that fairness in journalism could be combined with active partisanship in politics. Claude Bowers proudly recalled in his autobiography, *My Life*, that, while an editorial writer for the New York *World*, he wrote speeches for Democratic senatorial candidate Robert Wagner while running daily editorials in Wagner's support. As Ronald Steel recounts in his biography

Walter Lippmann and the American Century, Lippmann and James Reston in 1945 helped write a speech for Republican Sen. Arthur Vandenberg in which he broke from his isolationism. Lippmann then praised the turnabout in his column. Reston wrote a front page story on the speech in *The New York Times*, noting the "unusual interest" it attracted and observing that Sen. Vandenberg presented his theme "with force." President-elect John F. Kennedy shared with Lippmann a draft of his inaugural address. Lippmann proposed some modest changes that Kennedy accepted. After the new president delivered his speech, Lippmann praised it in his column as a "remarkably successful piece of self-expression." When George Will helped Ronald Reagan prepare for his television debates with Jimmy Carter in 1980 and then as an ABC commentator discussed Reagan's performance, he acted in a well-developed tradition.

With such intimate political involvement from leading lights of the journalism establishment, it is difficult to accept journalists' claims of political innocence—even the claims of journalists, like *Washington Post* editor Leonard Downie, who forswear voting for fear it could taint their scrupulous neutrality. But scrupulous accuracy and fairness are indeed the watchwords of journalistic competence today, even though the work of editorial writers, columnists and sports reporters (who are obliged to write from the viewpoint of the home team) offers countercurrents to professional ideals of detachment.

In the 1960s and again in the 1990s, some journalists have rebelled at the voicelessness of objective reporting and seek to write with an edge or an attitude that calls attention to the story as a piece of writing, not just a neutral vessel for transporting purportedly raw reality to audiences. Cutthroat competition encourages this. So does a postmodern relativism that spits at pretensions to objectivity.

At the same time, journalists, when criticized, invariably return to the old standbys. They assert their accuracy, their impartiality and their intrepid willingness to pursue the truth without fear or favor. There is safety in this. There is also honor: honor in the abnegation rather than the aggrandizement of self, and honor in the ordinary ambition to pursue a craft well rather than pursue art or influence badly.

As for Monica Lewinsky, the tender morsel on the fork of this season's feeding frenzy, there are certainly questions of journalistic fairness. (Did the press jump to conclusions that President Clinton and Ms. Lewinsky had an affair?) There are also questions about fairness and propriety in the special prosecutor's office. (Has the special prosecutor's office exceeded its mandate or encouraged leaks in a partisan effort to embarrass President Clinton?) The larger question about the news media, however, concerns not fairness but proportion. The press rushed to judgment not in asking whether the president violated his marriage vows, but in asking whether the very survival of his presidency would rest on this. There are no journalism school classes in prognostication, but a lot of reporters were dusting off their crystal balls in January or asking sources to consult theirs.

Outside Washington, this seemed nutty. Out here in the provinces, *Primary Colors* had been a best-seller. Out here in the boondocks, we had read about Paula Jones for years. Monica Lewinsky was a new name, but what she represented was old news. Journalists seemed to abandon not fairness but mental equilibrium. Washington seems to be a strange small town where local gossips do not whisper over the backyard fence but carry cell phones to call the *Times*. The one thing that the news media require to keep a sense of balance is a few moments of time for reflection. And that, it seems, is in short supply when the modern communicator is never disconnected.

At the same time there is a growing anxiety around journalism, if not inside it, that professional nonpartisanship, even at its best, has faults as well as virtues. Nonpartisanship hides informational cues that citizens need to make sense of complex issues. When a news story is written so that the readers do not know whether to cheer or boo, this represses emotional identification with political issues, persons and parties. Since nearly everyone today acknowledges that the organized political party has been a boon to democratic government, journalism that is divorced from parties and asserts a professional distrust of partisanship may help undermine one of the basic institutions of democracy.

Journalists are not about to rearm with partisan cudgels. The day of party loyalty is quite clearly over in American politics. But, then, is there any alternative to the distance that today's journalistic fairness places between politics and citizens? One possibility is "public journalism." Public journalists ask reporters not to abandon professional fairness for partisanship but to develop a kind of nonpartisan partisanship, an advocacy not of party loyalty but of public life. Public journalists want to use the news media to get citizens to talk to one another; they see no virtue in a journalistic chastity that keeps democracy's juices from flowing. It is too soon to know whether public journalism can develop a coherent set of professional norms and values itself, and the ideologues of conventional professionalism may well cut short its experimental fervor. We have yet to see.

Is modern professional fairness better for democracy, on balance, than the partisan press? So far as I know, no one has ever seriously studied this question. There are few studies that compare, say, party-oriented European journalism with objectivity-oriented American journalism, and none that successfully answer the tricky question of which serves democracy better. Do citizens know more about politics and vote more often where there is a party press or an independent press? In most European democracies, there is higher voter turnout and higher scores on tests of political knowledge than in the United States. But in Europe there are also stronger political parties and very different electoral institutions. What their effect might be on the values that direct the news media is simply unknown.

There is something enduring about the desire to be fair in journalism—both the writer's quest to be believed and the news institution's strong interest in maintaining its own credibility. But there is nothing at all stable across history or across national cultures about the actual rules and practices that pass for fairness. Today's journalistic fairness in the United States is a blend of high hopes, historic traditions, contemporary political culture and the expediencies journalists face in keeping audiences, owners and sources at bay. It is a shifting set of principles and practices that will be tested and reformulated by a changing informational environment whose shape will not hold still.

Michael Schudson, a 1985–86 Media Studies Center fellow, is a professor in the department of communication at the University of California, San Diego. He is author of The Power of News *and* The Good Citizen, *a study of the history of American public life (fall 1998).*

10

A Fall from Grace?

Daniel Hallin

Nobody elected the press, as the phrase goes. Journalism has become increasingly central to social and political life, but its legitimacy has always been open to question. Journalists point to the First Amendment, but the truth is that when it was written, neither large-scale media industries nor professional journalists existed, and the press had neither the independent economic foundation nor the privileged access to the halls of power that "the media" now enjoy. It is not surprising, then, that at many moments in American history, journalists have been accused of unfairness and abuse of power.

We are living today in one such moment. It is, perhaps, particularly painful to journalists, because it follows an unusual period during which the prestige of the news media was extremely high, and many believed that American journalism had found a solution to the traditional contradictions in the social role of the media—contradictions between private ownership and public responsibility and between the subjectivity of news judgment and the demand for objectivity.

This period can be dated roughly from the end of World War II through the mid-1970s to the mid-1980s. This was the era of "high modernism" in American journalism: It was a time when the belief ran strong that a professional elite could report the news rationally, without bias or subjectivity, that it could serve all of American society and indeed all of the Free World, that it could simultaneously be independent and firmly anchored in the institutional structure of society—equally a "watchdog" and a "fourth branch" of government. It was the heyday of the professional model of journalism, a period when the autonomy of the journalist within the news organization was relatively high. The separation of "church" and "state"—of journalism and the media business—was relatively strong, and it was widely accepted that journalism was first and foremost a "public trust."

Today the professional model of journalism has substantially broken down. It hasn't disappeared altogether, of course, and it probably never will: Some version of journalistic professionalism is probably unavoidable in a pluralistic society with a privately owned media system. There will always be a market for it, at least in a segment of the population that follows public affairs regularly and wants reliable, substantial information. And even those media that serve the mass public are likely to find professionalism a necessary refuge when charges of unfairness and irresponsibility become too loud. But the prestige, autonomy and privilege that the professional journalist enjoyed during the high-modernist era, as I argued in "Commercialism and Professionalism in the American News Media" (an essay in *Mass Media and Society*, edited by James Curran and Michael Gurevich), rested on very special historical circumstances. They may never be repeated.

Historic changes in the economics of the news media, combined with transformations in American politics, culture and society, have combined to erode those special circumstances. Journalistic professionalism had its heyday in an era when commercial pressures were limited. The three television networks enjoyed a stable oligopoly, FCC regulations imposed the obligation to serve the "public convenience and necessity," and network news divisions were largely insulated from the pressures of the rest of commercial television. Most newspapers had monopolies in their major markets—as they do today—but readership remained high, and most were insulated by family ownership from the pressures of Wall Street. Today deregulation and increased competition have eroded the barriers between journalism and media marketing, and as they have done so it has become harder for journalists to claim they are acting as holders of a public trust.

At the same time, a complex set of changes in political, social and cultural life has combined to further undercut the professional model.

Political authority has declined. The journalist of the high-modernist era solved the problem of his own authority to a large extent by borrowing from government officials: When the television reporter stood in front of the little flags in the State Department lobby and told us what "officials here believe," we trusted him, because we trusted them. Trust in public officials began to decline after 1964. The reasons are complex. Vietnam and Watergate no doubt played central roles, along with the divisions that accompanied social movements and counter-movements of this era, and the economic shocks that began in the 1970s. We should not forget that the high level of trust enjoyed by political authorities in the 1950s was not a "normal" historical condition but the product of specific and unusual circumstances—the legacy of the New Deal and World War II, the "national security" culture of the Cold War and economic affluence. The decline of public confidence in political authority undercut the old model of "objective reporting," which amounted most of the time to taking official statements at face value, forcing journalists to interpret the news more—and left them open to the kind of charges of bias and abuse of authority that Spiro Agnew began to hurl in the early 1970s. It also created increasing tension for journalists about whether to present themselves as insiders to the power structure or as populist outsiders.

The post-World War II consensus declined. The years after 1945 were a period of relative political consensus (or, if one likes, conformity). New Deal liberalism was ascendant in domestic politics. But real journalistic prestige lay in reporting foreign affairs and "national security"; it was in this sphere, above all, that bipartisanship reigned, and the national interest was assumed to be something on which all could agree. Today, domestic issues dominate the political agenda, partisan conflict—if not always real political debate—is sharper, and government is divided. This makes it far harder for journalists to present themselves as standing above partisan divisions.

New social movements, multiculturalism and identity politics have broadened and complicated the social and political landscape. Beginning with the civil rights movement and continuing through the Chicano movement, the women's movement, the gay and environmental movements and the rise—to some extent in reaction to these—of the religious right, social movements have heightened our consciousness of the cultural roots of news judgments. Consequently, the illusion of professional neutrality has been weakened.

The barrier between public and private has eroded. When journalists needed to reach Wendell Willkie, the Republican nominee for president in 1940, and couldn't find him at home, they called him at the apartment of Irita Van Doren, the literary editor of the *New York Herald Tribune*, with whom he had a long-running affair. Of course, no one would have considered reporting on that affair. Today, however, the shakiest rumor is likely to find its way into print. The change is often attributed to commercialization and the influence of tabloid news, and certainly that is an important factor. But it isn't the whole story. The Clinton/Monica Lewinsky sex scandal, for example, has been driven less by the tabloids than by the traditional press corps in Washington—for the political community inside the beltway far more than for the mass public.

Washington, for one thing, has become less clubby. There has been a shift, as political scientist Sam Kernell puts it, from "institutionalized pluralism" to "individualized pluralism," and the political game has become more savage as norms and leadership hierarchies have broken down. Meanwhile, the women's movement introduced the idea that "the personal is political," undermining codes of silence that protected certain forms of male power, presenting journalists and our society at large with genuinely difficult questions about where the boundary of publicity legitimately lies.

Whatever its causes, the eroding boundary between public and private also undermines the professional model: It tarnishes the journalist's aura of high-mindedness and statesmanship, and it thrusts the subjectivity of news judgments to the fore. In the Clinton/Lewinsky case, certainly, journalists' judgment about the importance of the affair diverged sharply from that of the public.

Sex scandals are only the most dramatic example of the dilemmas journalists face over news judgment. Many other kinds of stories that the men with the green eye shades would have regarded as "soft" news not fit for the front page—stories about what we could call the politics of everyday life—compete for the front page with the four-alarm fires and political press conferences of old. In some cases, the new and "soft" stories are run merely for their "infotainment" value, but in many cases they have legitimately expanded our understanding of what constitutes a public issue.

Simultaneous with all these changes, journalists have become in many ways more central as mediators of political and cultural life than ever before. In politics, for instance, the shift in the 1970s to a nomination system based on primary elections rather than party organizations made the news media increasingly important as an electoral battleground. At the same time, journalists themselves were becoming more active as mediators of news, moving away from the passive forms of reporting that prevailed in the 1950s and early 1960s, to write in ways that were often more interpretive and subjective. This shift began as a development within the practice of journalistic professionalism: As early as the 1950s, journalists had already started to worry about the ways in which "objective journalism" could leave them open to manipulation, as for instance in their coverage of Joe McCarthy. Eventually the rise of more aggressive techniques of news management, coupled with the collapse of political consensus and authority in the Vietnam/Watergate era, pushed them significantly in the direction of more analytical reporting.

Commercialization, meanwhile, also pushes in a parallel direction. Tabloid television, for example, jettisons the ethic of objectivity for one of emotional involvement: The journalist must show that he or she shares the emotions of the viewer. And at the magazine programs that have become the primary product of the network news divisions, it has become the conventional wisdom that a story needs a point of view to connect with the audience. At newspapers the change is more subtle; still, subjective styles of writing are widely seen as brightening up the paper and have clearly become more common.

The upshot is that journalists took on an increasingly active and central role at exactly the same time that conditions were making that role increasingly problematic.

Should we mourn the passing of the high-modernist era in American journalism as a decline of public life? Or should we celebrate it as the dawn of a more democratic age of multiple voices and responsiveness to popular taste? The answer, I think, is complex.

I have never been convinced by the view, held by many veteran journalists, that the changes of the last two decades represent a decline from the "golden age" of journalism. The professional model that prevailed during the post-World War II period was deeply problematic in many ways: It was (and often still is) overly entangled with the culture of official Washington, narrow in its conceptions of newsworthiness, naive in its assumption that the professional journalist could rise above the cultural and political biases that affect the rest of us. In 1992, when the second of the three presidential debates was organized in a "talk-show format," with citizens rather than journalists questioning the candidates, many journalists thought that this was a show-business perversion of the democratic process, that only they were qualified to represent the public intelligently. In fact, the talk-show format seemed to give the public a sense of participation they normally lacked. And they did a perfectly good job asking questions, quizzing the candidates on public policy, while the journalists, when they were back in charge for the third debate, focused on scandal and political strategy.

I am also not convinced by the view that journalistic professionalism is pure elitism and ought to be buried altogether. This view, inter-

estingly enough, is expressed in its purest form by an odd pair of intellectual bedfellows, both suspicious of the notion of the public interest to which professionalism appeals: neo-liberals, who celebrate the market, and certain postmodernists who see tabloid news as a site of popular resistance to elite domination. But professionalism never was pure elitism, even in the high-modernist period. It was important, for example, in limiting the ability of media owners to manipulate the political content of the news, something that may become increasingly important as multimedia conglomerates with wide-ranging political interests grow. It insisted that many troubling facts the marketers might have preferred to sweep under the rug of "happy news" had to be reported.

It is neither possible nor desirable to return to the high-modernist "golden age." Journalistic professionalism will have to change to survive. It will have to become less arrogant, more responsive, more willing to acknowledge multiple judgments and interpretations. But some version of a professional ethic is surely essential if journalism is to preserve its credibility. As marketplace logic has become dominant, it is increasingly common to hear journalists say they have no choice about the judgments they make because the sovereign consumer will not "sit still" for anything else.

But public reactions to the news are more complex than the consumer sovereignty view suggests. People may indeed watch the latest sex scandal or high-speed freeway chase. At the same time, they have opinions of their own about the public interest and about what constitutes responsible journalism, and they know a lack of integrity when they see it. As Robert M. Hutchins' Commission on Freedom of the Press suggested fifty years ago, the logic of the market and the logic of citizenship are not the same, and a media system that serves only the former is sure to come under criticism eventually. The professionalism of the high-modernist period was one solution to the problem, but a highly particular solution, the social conditions for which no longer exist. The problem is still very real, however, and a new solution will have to be found.

Daniel Hallin, a 1991–92 Media Studies Center fellow, is chair and professor in the department of communication at the University of California, San Diego. He is author of We Keep America on Top of the World: Television Journalism and the Public Sphere.

11

The Hutchins Commission,
Half a Century On—I

Andie Tucher

The Hutchins Commission on Freedom of the Press was that bunch
of pointy-heads who threatened to sic the government on the press if it
didn't behave itself—right? Wrong.

It was an uneven contest from the first, that clash of critiques between the professors and the press. Though it isn't entirely true that the
press greeted the Hutchins report in 1947 with a united front of deri-
sion, defiance and disgust, still the image of the Commission as feck-
less dilettantes willing to trample on the First Amendment has proved
remarkably durable as a shorthand description of the group and its work.
It's also inaccurate. Floated at the time, with greater or lesser vehe-
mence, by stalwarts ranging from *Editor & Publisher* and the dean of
Northwestern's Medill School of Journalism to the outspoken *Chicago
Tribune*—while at its annual meeting the American Society of Newspaper Editors decided they wouldn't even dignify the report by publi-
cizing their misgivings about it—the characterization was in large part
a propaganda triumph, a strategic strike in an ongoing battle between
the newspaper industry and the government.

It was true that most of the commissioners were ivory-tower intellectuals, with not a working journalist (let alone a working stiff) on the
formidable—even intimidating—roster. The work was inspired by
Henry Luce, publisher of *Time* magazine, but to carry it out he enlisted
his friend Robert M. Hutchins, chancellor of the University of Chicago
and onetime *wunderkind*. Hutchins assembled a group made up entirely of professors, ex-professors (the one apparent ringer, Federal
Reserve Chairman Beardsley Ruml, was a former Chicago dean) and

Archibald MacLeish, a poet who at the time of his appointment was librarian of Congress. All except MacLeish were comfortably ensconced either in the Ivy League, at the University of Chicago or at institutions in New York. All were white, male and eminent; the names of several, including Reinhold Niebuhr and Arthur M. Schlesinger Sr., are still recognized as leaders in their fields.

And the Commission did indeed raise the specter of government intervention. Freedom of the press, the report stated forthrightly, while "essential to political liberty," was in serious danger because of failures, abuses and derelictions on the part of its most powerful owners, and the agencies of the press "must control themselves or be controlled by government."

Yet despite screaming headlines in the press (Hutchins himself later recalled in one of his books an editorial in Albany's *Knickerbocker News* headed "Professors Blindly Try to Curb Press by Regulations to End All Our Liberties"), despite the claims of the *Tribune* that most of Hutchins' group had ties to the Communists, the Commission never intended, and never recommended, that government be given any control over what the press should be permitted to publish. In fact, after the passage quoted above about controlling the agencies of the press, the very next sentence was this: "If they are controlled by government, we lose our chief safeguard against totalitarianism—and at the same time take a long step toward it."

The press's charge that the Commission wanted to interfere with its rights was actually something of a red herring floated to divert attention from the group's greatest concern: not so much content as concentration. Hutchins' report focused on the fact that the press had become a big business—"an enormous and complicated piece of machinery"— concentrated in the hands of a few wealthy moguls who ruled their empires with little concern for the needs, wants or welfare of the public.

It was not a new complaint. Press critics and the general public had for years been charging that the press lords were arrogant, remote and much more conservative than most of their readers, particularly as evidenced by their consistent and overwhelming support for whoever was running *against* Franklin D. Roosevelt.

And the era's press moguls were indeed legendary. William Randolph Hearst was by then over 80 and had lost some of his empire and much of his power in a financial shake-up a decade earlier. But many still remembered when his ambition had seemed a juggernaut. In just four years, from 1902 to 1906, he had won two elections to Congress and lost one each for president (coming in second to Alton Parker at the Democratic nominating convention), mayor of New York City and governor of New York. He had been denounced as pro-German during World War I and had been a rabid crusader against the Reds after it. Generally considered the model for Orson Welles' megalomaniac *Citizen Kane* when the movie was released in 1941, Hearst confirmed the popular impression by refusing to review the movie in any of his publications.

Col. Robert McCormick was still going strong. Though his empire was smaller than Hearst's, his flagship *Chicago Tribune* had an influence that was enormous and, in the eyes of many observers, malign. As A.J. Liebling put it in 1947, "Bertie is always good for a laugh, like the word Brooklyn in a radio script.... [But] the *Tribune* circulation remains more than a million weekdays, a million and a half Sundays, and people who read it acquire a habit, not of agreeing with Colonel McCormick, which would be almost impossible, but of thinking of anybody slightly less reactionary than the colonel as a liberal." A famous Roosevelt hater, during the 1936 campaign the Colonel was reported to have instructed his switchboard operators to answer the phone with "Good morning, *Chicago Tribune*. There're only 43 (or less) days left in which to save the American way of life."

Yet despite the enormous power of these and other owners, for most of the century the newspaper industry had been left almost entirely unfettered; the higher courts had by and large declined to interfere, tacitly agreeing with the owners' premise that any attempt to regulate even the business side of the press would be an infringement on First Amendment rights. Only recently had the coming of the Depression and the election of Roosevelt changed all that. Suddenly the Fourth Estate found itself subject, like any builder of autos or slaughterer of chickens, to the ministrations of Dr. New Deal. In the late 1930s and early '40s the Supreme Court handed down a series of decisions declaring that traditional values of press freedom did not free the press from submission to interstate commerce regulations, antitrust laws and wage-and-hour codes.

It wasn't just newspapers, either, that were squirming under the suddenly heavy hand of government. The Federal Communications Commission wrangled for years with NBC, CBS, the National Association of Broadcasters and Congress over whether the big radio networks, by controlling so many of the available high-power stations, were operating as monopolies. So rancid grew the battle that Martin Dies' House Committee on Un-American Activities scoured the FCC for subversives, and another powerful congressman, Eugene Cox of Georgia, attacked FCC Chairman James Lawrence Fly himself, whom he called "the most dangerous man in Washington," for using Gestapo tactics—a resonant charge indeed in 1942. (Fly fought back with style, at one point remarking that the NAB reminded him of "a dead mackerel in the moonlight—it both shines and stinks.")

The Supreme Court finally ended the battle in 1943 by upholding the FCC's demand that NBC divest itself of one of its two networks, which was bought by the Life Savers candy magnate Edward J. Noble for $8 million and turned into ABC. And a year after the report was issued, the Supreme Court would turn its attention to the movies, agreeing with the government that the studios should divest themselves of their substantial interest in the theaters that showed the films they produced.

Yet the press's operatic alarm over the Commission's intentions, besides being a tad Machiavellian, was also, apparently, unnecessary. Hutchins' group, despite its grave concerns that the concentration of ownership was limiting the variety of news and sources available to the public—despite this record of government regulation and the clear pleasure the Roosevelt administration was taking in anything that might bridle its critics—nonetheless chose to recommend great caution in the application of antitrust laws to the press.

Such laws, the report pointed out, "can be very dangerous to the freedom and the effectiveness of the press. They can be used to limit voices in opposition and to hinder the processes of public education." Commission member Zechariah Chafee, a Harvard professor of law, included in his supplementary report on "Government and Mass Communications" a chapter recalling the members' musings on the question "Is Bigness Badness?" They declined to determine that it was. "The real problem," they concluded, "is how to give more power to the people who are professionally motivated and less to the people who are economically or profit motivated."

The hijacking of the report by its most obsessed and vociferous critics had unfortunate consequences for the Commission's aspirations. The report included plenty of suggestions and critiques that had nothing to do with either government control or the lack thereof, and most of its general recommendations to improve the performance of the press were intelligent and sound. The press should be responsible, the Commission said. The press should be accountable. The press should not lie. The press should facilitate public discussion, inform citizens of the opinions and attitudes of other groups, present and clarify society's goals, and reach every citizen. But discussion of these ideals was all but eclipsed by the phantom issue of government intervention.

Nor did anyone at the time address the most intriguing reverberation from the Commission's clearly professorial bent: not their limited real-world experience in journalism but their choice to criticize journalists in a language few real-world journalists used or even seemed familiar with. It was an almost elegaic language, resonant of the bygone era in which most of the Commission members had grown up—that sunnier age before World War I when official mainstream culture rested on the premise that moral laws were eternal and universally applicable, that if people were clearly shown the differences between right and wrong they would inevitably choose the right, that humankind would continue to progress, that a bunch of smart men sitting around talking could solve almost any social ill.

The report is full of words like "morality," "conscience" and "obligation," and they are used entirely without irony. The agencies of the press served a moral purpose, it said, because "if a man is burdened with an idea, he not only desires to express it; he ought to express it. He owes it to his conscience and the common good." But, it went on to say, "[i]n the absence of accepted moral duties there are no moral rights." And the Commission described its decision not to invoke legal remedies in these words: "It is not even desirable that the whole area of the responsible use of freedom should be made legally compulsory, even if it were possible; for in that case free self-control, a necessary ingredient of any free state, would be superseded by mechanism."

It was a noble effort, rooted in a vision of culture that did, for all its naiveté and even paternalism, nourish a refreshing optimism about the possibilities for improvement—not just of journalism but of humankind, too. But if they noticed this language at all, most of the targets of the Commission's report were more irritated than enlightened. Fortune magazine was speaking for many when it labeled the report "difficult" and "exasperating"; other critics complained it was vague, ambiguous, overly academic, overly condensed—even dull. The most serious indictment of the press of 1947 might be that so much of it looked at the report and, willfully or not, just didn't get it.

Now, half a century after its publication, can a critique written in a premodern idiom, analyzing the press of a pretelevision, pre-Internet, pre-O.J. era, have any conceivable relevance to a generation even more inclined to quirk an eyebrow upon hearing the word "moral"?

Much of what has happened since 1947 would appall the Commission. The increasing concentration of power, the increasing trend toward "big business" the group so feared, has progressed to such an extent that to a '90s eye the Commission's fears seem almost quaint. Not only have the communications empires ballooned in size, most of them have also become subempires in even larger conglomerates that girdle the globe and include under one umbrella businesses that have nothing to do with journalism, businesses ranging from defense contracting to financial services—businesses that have been traditional investigative targets of the very journalists who are now their corporate cousins and siblings.

Of the "Big Five" book publishers named in the 1947 report, one folded years ago and the other four have been swallowed by global conglomerates; of the "Big Eight" movie studios, one has faded away and the others have been merged and sold and remerged and resold to megacorporations or investors; of the "Big Four" television networks, Mutual has vanished and we all know what happened to the other three.

When the mighty mogul Hearst was "at the top of his fortunes" a few years earlier, said the report, he owned 26 newspapers, 13 magazines, eight radio stations, a newsreel company, the King Features syndicate, the International News Service and an interest in MGM. The iconic moguls for the '90s include Rupert Murdoch, who owns properties on five continents—among them 125 newspapers, two magazines, including the huge-circulation *TV Guide*, one U.S. broadcast network, 22 U.S. television stations, the Fox News Channel, Fox Sports, the Twentieth Century Fox studio, the HarperCollins publishing company and the Los Angeles Dodgers—and who has already pressured HarperCollins and his Asia-based satellite network to help pimp his courtship of the vast Chinese market. Then there's Bill Gates, whose ambitions are so naked that a Web hoaxster's widely circulated report announcing Microsoft's purchase of the Vatican was almost too plausible to be funny. Whether either mogul is now "at the top of his fortunes" or merely preparing to scale even greater heights is an open question.

The choice to use the regulatory powers of the government has also grown much less fashionable. The Justice Department's investigation of Microsoft has been most notable for its rarity, and the Telecommunications Act of 1996, which President Clinton declared would increase competition and allow "our laws [to] catch up with the future," has simply permitted the colossal empires to contemplate a future nothing short of stupendous.

Some of what the Commission feared has *not* happened—though that may not be entirely to the good. The group, concerned about the steady decline in the "number of units" of communication available to disseminate the news, feared a continual shrinkage in the amount of information available. But while the rise of the Internet, which can make a journalist of anybody who knows HTML coding, has certainly broadened public access to information, the reporting on the Monica Lewinsky story poses a real challenge to the Commission's sanguine conviction that "the cure for distorted information would seem to be more information, not less."

Some of what the Commission recommended *has* happened—and backfired. In 1947 the press was scathing about the group's decision to consider film, magazines and radio on the same plane as newspapers as agencies of mass communication that ought to share both the responsibilities and protections of the First Amendment. Yet while the term "mass media" has now grown elastic enough to embrace those genres and more, the idea of responsibility has simply drooped like an old garter taxed by a thickening thigh, and the language of commerce, not accountability, has become the Esperanto of the modern media.

To take just one small example, during the month of February alone the daily "Media Circus" column of the on-line 'zine *Salon* turned its sights on, among other topics, the Academy Award nominations, *Spy* magazine, the Yiddish weekly *Forward*, the on-line search engine Lycos, a trashy detective bestseller, CBS's Olympics coverage and the new Absolut vodka ad. Maintaining the values and standards of journalism—let alone arguing persuasively that such things exist—is hard enough in an age when many readers lump *The Washington Post* in the same category as the Drudge Report. But what meaningful conclusions could be drawn about the values of a category that included the *Post*, the gossipmonger and the martini?

Some of the commission's recommendations have however been successfully adopted—like its call for more open and pointed criticism of the press's performance. The Nieman Foundation at Harvard began publishing its series of *Reports* in direct response to the Commission's demand, other journalism reviews have been founded, and independent "academic-professional centers of advanced study, research and publication in the field of communications" have been established.

Even the press itself does more of the kind of "vigorous mutual criticism" of its own foibles that the Commission suggested—but again with mixed results. Many responsible news organizations do indeed take pains to admit their own mistakes, and many take even greater pains to point out their rivals'. But especially for sensational and competitive stories like the Lewinsky saga, the "has the press gone too far?" piece has become just another inevitable entry in the standard cycle. We know that Ted Koppel will devote a "Nightline" to it, that *The New York Times* will turn out lengthy sidebars on it, that journalists will parade their distaste for having to air the most lurid details (like this one, and this one, and then, oh, this one!), and that virtually no one will say, "You know what? We really *have* gone too far this time."

Which suggests that in the end, the most compelling legacy of the Hutchins report and the best argument for the survival of that gently old-fashioned language of morality may be a simple benchmark test for assessing the state of journalistic credibility and performance.

If enough readers and viewers can hear the words "journalism," "morality" and "values" in the same sentence without quirking an eyebrow, the press is on the right track.

Andie Tucher is the author of Froth and Scum: Truth, Beauty, Goodness, and the Ax-Murder in America's First Mass Medium.

12

The Hutchins Commission,
Half a Century On—II

Mark N. Trahant

The first time I read the Hutchins Commission report, it was like reading Plato on journalism—a philosophical framework to the craft. We have all heard, and I certainly believed, how important good journalism is to democracy. Hutchins makes that case too and outlines five minimum requirements for that to occur. But if Hutchins is a philosophical guide, it's also a practical one. The ideas raised by the Commission are relevant and worth trying in a time when readers, viewers and citizens all ask, What are the standards of journalism? What does good journalism look like?

I thought the 50th anniversary of the Hutchins Commission's report a good reason to ask readers these very questions. In 1997, as editor and publisher of *the Moscow-Pullman* (Idaho) *Daily News*, a small afternoon newspaper distributed in two university towns on the Idaho/Washington border, I wrote a 12-part series exploring ideas raised by Hutchins. I published one essay a month for one year. I used the philosophical framework of Hutchins to look at how our newspaper practices journalism, from local coverage to what we publish from national sources. We looked at how journalism was practiced in the past and worked forward.

The series had a local angle from its first chapter. Robert Maynard Hutchins, the chairman and inspiration for the Commission, visited Moscow in 1956. He came here despite a call for a boycott from the American Legion, which charged that Hutchins was soft on communism. Record crowds showed up to listen to the famous educator anyway, according to newspaper accounts. Hutchins thanked the American Legion for performing a valuable public service because it had called attention to the First Amendment. "It is the duty to defend these principles for which this country stands," Hutchins said at the Moscow Hotel. "And these are the real strength of America. Without these, it is merely a piece of land between Canada and Mexico."

In that spirit, I looked back at our past. My essays reviewed coverage of sensational crimes, such as the Lindbergh trial, a passport fraud trial involving a local religious leader who once owned this newspaper and the O.J. Simpson case. In 1936, *Daily News-Review* (as the paper was then called) headline writers said the kidnapping and murder of Charles A. Lindbergh Jr. was the "Crime of the Century." All the twists and turns of the story and the trial were big news, often taking more than half of the front page (as well as six-column, 200-point headlines). So too was the trial of Dr. Frank Robinson, the founder of a local religious group, Psychiana. Robinson also happened to own the newspaper, so it was deemed important when the British expatriate was accused of passport fraud. It was a six-column, 200-point banner when he was acquitted in May of 1936. In presenting historical examples of crime and courtroom stories from our paper, my essays offered our readers a different perspective on the O.J. Simpson trial—a trial that was not extensively covered in our pages.

I also looked at ways in which the newspaper transmitted society's values. During World War II the masthead included the phrase "For a New Day of Independence and Liberty—Buy Those Extra War Bonds!" But society's values had changed by the Vietnam era—and again this newspaper reflected that. On July 5, 1968, the front page had four stories about the war effort: two reports from the battlefield and two reports about student protests. Instead of promoting war bonds, the editorial page suggested the war was not going well, citing the old story: My dog would have won, if it wasn't for the other dog.

My twelve essays looked back at issues raised by Hutchins, examined how this newspaper covered similar stories and then asked how we might do better in the future. The essays were complemented by exchanges conducted by telephone, letters, e-mail and public meetings about the practice of journalism in our community.

Readers of the *Daily News* eagerly joined in a conversation. During the course of the series, more than 500 readers wrote letters or e-mailed pointed suggestions about what this community's journalism standards ought to be. Another 200 telephoned, visited the newspaper or participated in community meetings. What makes those numbers remarkable is that they total more than 10 percent of our subscriber list.

As an afternoon newspaper, we told readers that we were shifting our resources away from events and toward issues. We weren't giving up on events—we would continue to note them—but we would try to use the Hutchins test of context to give stories meaning. News stories with context means reporters need more time. We did this by covering fewer stories in the daily report in exchange for depth.

Some readers say that means we quit covering "news." A.S. Cutting of Moscow wrote: "Ever since the name was changed from the Idahonian to this present name [*Moscow-Pullman Daily News*], the quality has degraded to the bottom. The old name was the only one in the world and this one is all over the world.... so about the only local news can be found in the obituary section." However, Robert Johnson of Pullman wrote: "I am greatly enthusiastic about your approach; it is sure to make the *News* a better paper. Fleshing the story out, journalism with content are what we need."

Even the readers who did not come to meetings or write letters were interested in Hutchins—and a better newspaper. One night a *Daily News* columnist was hosting a local charity event when she took advantage of the microphone to tease me about my zeal regarding the "Hutchinson" Commission. By the end of the dinner, four different readers went to the columnist to chide her, "You know it's really the Hutchins Commission."

The series showed how our newspaper could improve by presenting readers with Hutchins' analysis of what America requires of the press: "Today, our society needs, first, a truthful, comprehensive, and intelligent account of the day's events in a context which gives them meaning; second, a forum for the exchange of comment and criticism; third, a means of projecting the opinions and attitudes of the groups in the society to one another; fourth, a method of presenting and clarifying the goals and values of the society; and, fifth, a way of reaching every member of the society by the currents of information, thought, and feeling which the press supplies."

In 1947, the Commission argued that America's requirements of the press "are greater in variety, quantity, and quality than those of any previous society in any age." The statement was obvious then. Today it takes on additional meaning because of the frenetic pace of society and the news media. Most of the images broadcast or printed these days are likely to be entertaining versions of events rather than what the Hutchins Commission called "full access to the day's intelligence."

Yet this very requirement may be the most difficult standard for a community newspaper. What is full access to the day's intelligence? In the series we looked at the newspaper's history before answering that question. A former editor recalled what journalism was like a decade earlier in the 1950s: "I had a rule of 25 stories on page 1. Now they run four stories on page 1," Louis A. Boas wrote. He admitted a preference for short stories over long ones because "I don't think one person in 50 reads the whole thing except those about whom it is written or their friends."

Today, we generally run four stories on the front page. All of them are longer than those of earlier generations. Nevertheless, many readers said they preferred short stories and demanded more depth. Is this a contradiction? I think not. In a newspaper the trick is to note the inconsequential and the routine yet save time and space for the larger questions.

For example, Moscow and Pullman—two rural university towns—are at the beginning of a major societal shift as more and more young people attend school at urban campuses instead of going away to college. About five years ago, the on-campus student population went flat. More recently it has started to shrink by a few percentage points each year. A few businesses, landlords and others complain about the schools' smaller population. This trend portends a very different type of community here in five, 10 or 20 years. Our newspaper is ideally suited to help explain what is occurring. Even better, we can help readers explore the meaning of these changes and provide what Hutchins calls a forum for exchange of comment and criticism.

Perhaps the most prescient section of *A Free and Responsible Press* is its discussion on race. Five decades ago this group of male scholars said journalism and, indeed, our democracy, would fail if we could not understand all of the different groups, racial and others, that make up America. Before the urban riots in the summer of 1967, which is when most newspapers discovered racial issues, the Hutchins Commission reasoned: "The account of an isolated fact, however accurate in itself, may be misleading and, in effect, untrue.... The country has many groups that are partially insulated from one another and that need to be interpreted to one another. Factually correct but substantially untrue accounts of the behaviors of members of one of these social islands can intensify the antagonisms of others toward them. A single incident will be accepted as a sample group action unless the press has given a flow of information and interpretation concerning the relations between two racial groups such as to enable the reader to set a single event in its proper perspective. If allowed to pass as a sample of such action, the requirement that the press present an accurate account of the day's events in a context which gives them meaning has not been met."

When I use this reasoning in community forums and speeches, people grasp its importance to all of us. I try to explain that for me the First Amendment is in part a vision of an America where we can respect differences and still build a country. The Hutchins report enlarges this idea because it shifts the discussion away from "minority" groups to "constituent" groups—making it clearer that we are all in this together. When I explained this in one of my sessions, a reader said it changed the way he thought about both the First Amendment and diversity issues.

Of course, the concept of constituent groups takes in much more than just racial groups. This was illustrated for us by our increased religion coverage. "I like the way you are covering more stories about religion, especially the ones I do not know about," one reader said, probably reflecting the majority of our readers. But two others saw the coverage completely differently: One canceled a subscription because "religion has become the major focus of your paper," and another quit because he said the paper had become so "anti-Christian and anti-religion."

The Hutchins Commission report also provides insights for understanding the relationship between news values and technology. The Commission predicted the personal newspaper delivered to readers by facsimile machine—an idea far ahead of its time. When Hutchins was published the authors noted that television was a promising medium, but said little else.

Today the Internet has emerged in its own right. We see its growing influence on society, the news media and our values. Perhaps it is the ideal time to see what notions from Hutchins might apply. Can the Internet be a medium of context that gives stories meaning? Absolutely. Moreover, the four other minimum requirements of Hutchins might even add credibility to new media reports.

The 50th anniversary of the Hutchins Commission was mostly ignored by the news media. And why not? The press has ignored or attacked the report since its publication. Most editors and publishers had a long list of complaints: They dismissed the extension of First Amendment rights to broadcasters, they disliked the idea of public participation in judging our standards, and they said the very idea of the Hutchins Commission could lead to government regulation of the news media. Worse still, publishers said they'd go broke if they followed the overly academic recommendations of Hutchins.

Yet Hutchins recognized the pressures of the marketplace—surely as great a problem today as it was then. Why can't market pressures be an incentive for innovation, self-examination and a challenge to be better than we are now?

Academic or not, five decades ago the Hutchins Commission showed us we can improve the news media by paying attention to our readers, listeners or viewers. This was the Commission's greatest hope because media consumers have immense power, as Margaret A. Blanchard wrote in a 1977 *Journalism Monographs* essay in which she said Hutchins' goal was "to educate and goad this silent audience into action."

I, too, hoped to reach this silent audience. In 1997, I was not sure where my Hutchins series would end. I thought readers might be interested in a local news council, a place where they could judge errors and remind us of our responsibilities. I was even prepared to help organize it. But the prospect of a local news council did not interest my readers. Instead, they favored a clearer definition of our newspaper's standards, a way to measure what we are doing against what we could be doing.

For the *Daily News*, the conversation with readers—letting them in on the definitions of good journalism—was what was important. Hutchins' five minimum requirements remain a fair test of what we publish and how that contributes to community.

Recently a reader called to complain about one of our daily stories about a "crime wave" in Pullman, essentially a few cars being broken into and small items stolen. He said: "That story did not meet the test of a context that gave the story meaning." The criticism was precise, and the language was directly from Hutchins. I felt like Plato was reading our paper.

Mark N. Trahant, a columnist for The Seattle Times, *is the former editor and publisher of the* Moscow-Pullman *(Idaho)* Daily News.

13

The Hutchins Commission,
Half a Century On—III

Lee C. Bollinger

It is curious that the Hutchins Commission report should be receiving as much attention as it has in the last few years. Curious because the report was fairly widely criticized when it first appeared in 1947 and then seemed to sink without a trace until this very recent surge of interest. As an illustration of the report's apparent insignificance, consider that only a handful of Supreme Court decisions have ever cited it, despite the fact that a major thrust of the report was directed towards evaluating the legal and constitutional status of the media. An opening question therefore might be, What has led to this revival?

A natural place to begin in answering that question is with the substance of the report. It is, in fact, one of the more powerfully expressed critiques of the press. Its central theme is about the tension between the "business" (sell as many papers as you can) and the "professional" (meet the needs of citizens to be informed) mentalities. The report's articulate denunciation of the media's increasing pandering to the baser desires of the population and its depiction of the media's noble role in a democratic society give it, in my view, the potential to be an enduring document. It is, to be sure, rather slight in its analysis. (What exactly do we mean by "professional"? Why should the press think it knows better than the people what they should receive as "news"?) The tone of the report may at times come across as smug and elitist, and it is short in specific remedies. Although it calls for a permanent, nongovernmental commission to conduct an ongoing review of the press, the report mostly confines itself to threatening the press with a loss of its sacred privilege of constitutional liberty, without ever saying what legal remedies might appropriately be applied if it does not reform itself. Still, when all is said and done, the likely source of the current revival of interest in the report is to be found in its fundamental criticism of the media as out to make a buck at the expense of democracy.

One question to be asked is whether the situation today is better or worse than it was during the 1940s. Is the press better at living up to its noble role, or has it sunken even deeper in the quest to turn a profit? Since the report gives only anecdotes of pandering and no real empirical benchmarks for press performance, we really do not have any clear way of confidently answering that comparative question. Perhaps some might question whether the comparison is worth probing into—after all, it might be said that whether we're on a downward or an upward slope is largely irrelevant. What should matter to us is simply whether we think the media have fallen below some threshold standard. But a historical perspective can often be illuminating about underlying causes and conditions and about trends we might otherwise neglect. I think it useful to divide the period of time since the report into two parts—a several-decade-long perspective and the immediate or contemporary period we seem to be in right now.

In a long-term perspective, some things, it seems to me, are at least identifiably different about the context in which media operate today—differences that bear on the standards the report put forward as appropriate. Since the early post-World War II period, there have been arguably many significant changes. The Supreme Court, and the courts generally, have considered and greatly expanded the constitutional rights of the press under the First Amendment. What is significant about that fact is not just that the press has more freedom, but also that the courts have themselves become significant public speakers about articulating the role of the press in our society. And, in fact, the courts (and especially the Supreme Court) have again and again expressed a vision of the democratic role of the media very much like that put forward in the report. The Courts play a role in shaping our social norms, and so we now have an authoritative voice regularly addressing the function of the press in our political system. Moreover, on a number of occasions the courts have made it completely clear that constitutional rights will follow professional performance. (The degree of constitutional protection, for libelous utterances, for example, depends in part on whether the press is addressing public "controversies" or other matters.)

The emergence of the electronic media (radio, television and cable) in the postwar era also brought forth new developments that supported the themes in the Hutchins Commission report. One development was the creation of the system of public broadcasting, which was to embody precisely the kind of elevation of public discussions thought to be hindered by commercialism. For the past 40 years we witnessed a rise in public regulation of the electronic media, much of it designed to enhance the level of public discussion. Relying on the 1934 Communications Act and decades of congressional amendments, administrative regulations and judicial interpretations, the Federal Communications Commission, beginning in the 1960s, greatly expanded its attentions to the extent and "fairness" of coverage of controversial issues and candidacies for election to public office. While this body of public governance applied only to the electronic and not the print media, and while a good deal of it has vanished in the past decade, it nevertheless provided (arguably) a general standard for all media and at times functioned as a sword of Damocles ready to befall the print media should they too become lax in meeting the responsibilities of serving a higher public purpose.

Yet despite these significant thrusts in the direction advocated by the Commission's report, I sense that its fears about media under the thrall of commercial interests are all too present in our culture once again—and herein lies the primary reason for the renewal of interest in the Hutchins Commission report.

It is, of course, always difficult to try to capture a public mood, but some things are clear and support a felt sense that the ominous messages of the report are once again relevant. Certainly, the system of public broadcasting has been under siege in the last decade, and the worries about it succumbing to commercial pressures are not ungrounded. Furthermore, the scope of public regulation of the broadcast and electronic media have been almost wholly curtailed (the Fairness Doctrine, for example, was eliminated entirely by the FCC, acting out the philosophy of the Reagan administration), in favor of a market-oriented approach to meeting the "public interest." And, finally, while the Supreme Court has been supportive of First Amendment rights for the press in the last decades, there have not been the great First Amendment cases involving the press (such as *New York Times Co. v. Sullivan* or the Pentagon Papers case) in which the court has spoken to the great role of the media in advancing the nation's commitment to democracy.

Along with these shifts both in the behavior of the media and in the emergence of new technologies of communications, both of which are worrisome from a Hutchins Commission report perspective, there is a palpable sense in the society that, in the face of this general deregulation of the media and the triumph of a simple market approach, both the quantity and quality of coverage of public issues and concerns seem to be in decline. Invasions of privacy and a fixation on what used to be reduced to the level of gossip now seem on the ascendancy. To many there has been a fundamental shift in the threat to our Fourth Branch of government—from a threat of government censorship and coercion (reflected in our great First Amendment decisions such as *New York Times Co. v. Sullivan*) to a threat of commercial pressures producing a trivialization of media content. As the Commission wrote for its time, we too may be living with a constitutional and public policy regime created for a different world, one with concerns about preserving the sovereignty of the people from threat of government censorship, while today the threat is commercial degradation.

Meanwhile, we have the striking new development of computer technology. The speed and scope of coverage of the world is expanding exponentially. This brings all kinds of issues to a head: the potentially greater ease for sinister attitudes to flourish and the steady removal of citizens from the reality of lived experience. Does it matter, to put the issue somewhat more sharply, if violent hate groups now have Web pages?

Now, this thesis—that there is a growing sense of unease about a significant decline in the quality of public discussions of public issues in the media, encouraged by a commercial mentality—seems to me worth exploring, both in whether it reflects the society's mood or sense of the world and whether there is any foundation to it. I have long advocated another commission such as the Hutchins Commission, precisely because it seems there ought to be periodically (perhaps every decade) an independent, nongovernmental look at the media and its general course. It still seems to me a good idea.

Lee C. Bollinger is president of the University of Michigan, an authority on the First Amendment and author of Images of a Free Press *and* The Tolerant Society: Freedom of Speech and Extremist Speech in America.

14

The Impossibility of Fairness

Jim Squires

Establishing parameters of fairness in the age of cyberspace is no different from trying to set them fifty years ago at the *Chicago Tribune* or *The New York Times*. Each case is unique, and the debate always ends the way it did in the Victorian England of author Thomas Hughes.

"He never wants anything but what's right and fair," Hughes wrote of a character in *Tom Brown's Schooldays*, "only when you come to settle what's right and fair, it's everything that he wants, and nothing that you want."

Recollection of my own record starts with my treatment of a Nashville used-car salesman who committed suicide in the 1960s following my story of his pending indictment. *The* (Nashville) *Tennessean*, though entirely accurate, was unfair to the car dealer by singling him out for front-page notoriety. Not all those expected to be indicted by the grand jury that day were treated the same way.

I also wrote countless stories based on anonymous sources, and I was not once concerned about the racial, ethnic and gender balance of the sources I quoted. A great deal of my unfairness was rooted in my unavoidable personal profile as a Southern white male. In the broad sense that fairness by news media is now being debated in the public mind, it is possible that none of the zillion stories I wrote was fair.

Yet even the worst individual case of unfairness does not approach the level of injustice being perpetrated by the information industry as a whole. What could be more unfair to citizens than the outright corruption of journalism, which takes place daily in all quarters of the so-called news media?

With the exception of a few fine and committed newspapers and magazines, the professional standards and values of journalism have

71

gone to hell in a handbasket, cast out in favor of an entertainment culture with no moral compass and no concern for fairness—or taste.

Even at its worst and most unfair, the American brand of journalism once had as its goal a quest for accuracy and perspective that would eventually produce truth. News, which is the product of real journalism, was best defined by the Hutchins Commission on freedom of the press in 1947 as a "truthful, comprehensive, and intelligent account of the day's events in a context which gives them meaning."

Ostensibly, information was gathered, evaluated and eventually disseminated in the interest of enlightenment and education. Conversely, the consumers of journalism had good reason to believe that the purveyors of news existed to provide them a fair deal and a fair account. Journalism's value in the marketplace was its quality, of which fairness is a vital part. Like all the great products of American capitalism, brand-name integrity was its greatest asset. Shoddy, inferior news coverage invariably failed in the competitive marketplace. This is no longer true.

The broadcast industry is an entertainment industry to which news is purely incidental. It is primarily television's shoddy attempts at journalism, such as its injurious handling of the identification of the Atlanta Olympics bombing suspect, that have fueled the fairness controversy and spawned cries for press regulation. Print journalism used to routinely withhold the names of suspects until they had been charged. Even when one publication felt it necessary, others often restrained themselves, minimizing the damage. This is no longer possible when TV has a breathless correspondent, dressed like a cat burglar, camped outside the suspect's apartment, endlessly speculating live on camera about everything but the color of the man's underwear. "The bigger the lie, the louder the cry" has taken on new meaning in light of the instant global impact of a CNN bulletin or a report on the Internet.

Today television and movie producers, networks, cable operators and information providers of all stripes value "news" not for its importance, quality or public service contributions but for its ability to attract an audience and turn a profit. Thus, for today's press, the best story is a sex scandal such as the "bimbo eruptions" that have plagued President Clinton.

In a speech last year Harold Evans, the distinguished English author, editor and former president and publisher of Random House, quoted William S. Paley, founder of CBS, as saying that the day news becomes a profit center will be lamentable. "Well, the day has come," Evans said. "It's about dusk."

With the passing of time, the standards of journalism have been relaxed to the point of nonexistence. Yet news remains the favorite subject of the entertainment business to such an extent that the lines between news and entertainment have been forever obliterated. News
provides a steady stream of programming free of creative and promo-
tion costs. From the ABC and CNN coverage of the Iranian hostage
crisis to television's obsession with O.J. Simpson nearly twenty years
later, true stories have proven to be a sure ticket to ratings and profits.

Movies, television specials and even sitcoms are built around "news"
situations and actual events. Celebrity personalities are most often sub-
stituted for genuine newsmakers, but sometimes the newsmakers end
up getting hired by the news media and become celebrities themselves.
Accuracy in the retelling of their stories is, quite naturally, less important to scripts than excitement and audience appeal. People walk out of
movies like *JFK*, which purported to chronicle the conspiracy behind
the assassination of President Kennedy, or last year's fictional extrava-
ganza on the Titanic, and say in all seriousness, "I didn't know that."
Guess not, it never happened.

For today's press the "best news" combines sex and crime and prominent people, like O.J. Simpson and President Clinton. The actual events
become great television entertainment. Then they spawn books, which
are turned into movies, which attempt to make them even more entertaining than they were originally.

News events spawn new celebrities, who show up at a later event
with a microphone, pretending to practice the craft of journalism. Ac-
tors, comedians, politicians, lawyers, infamous criminals—and some
who fit all five categories—now regularly masquerade as reporters on
newscasts and talk shows. Watergate burglar G. Gordon Liddy and
Clinton White House political adviser George Stephanopoulos are both
now widely considered to be journalists. Former Nixon speechwriter
Patrick Buchanan and civil rights activist Jesse Jackson go from being
story subject one month to storyteller the next. Lawyer Johnnie Cochran
may be on television standing beside a famous defendant one day and
on another interviewing the same defendant from behind an anchor
desk.

Worse, many of the people signing the pay checks of these pretend-
ers and making the programming decisions can't see any difference
between real news and celebrity news programming. They think that
having been celebrated in one news event qualifies someone to cover
another. It never crosses their minds that their position in charge of

news organizations carries with it a responsibility to protect and preserve the values of real journalism.

Sadly, through acquisition and merger much of the real journalism
establishment has been swallowed up by the entertainment industry.
Some of the biggest, most important and powerful news organizations
in the world today are owned by companies whose main business is
make believe. The Cable News Network and Time magazine, for example, are controlled by the entertainment giant Time Warner, cable
owner, maker of HBO movies and producer of sleazy rap songs.

To grasp the implications of this for journalism and democracy, what
would happen if a strong grass-roots movement for media censorship
were ever mounted in this country? Its most just and likely targets would
be cable television pornography, the violence-profanity-sex formula
movies of HBO and Time Warner's abhorrent rap lyrics—all of which
trumpet the legally obscene F-word.

It is easy to imagine that Time Warner would raise its First Amendment shield and march behind it to Washington to oppose this assault on
its profit centers. So would many other major media companies with
whom Time Warner has significant financial dealings and mutual interests.

But would this be fair to the watchers of CNN, the readers of Time
and the customers of other journalism organizations with ties to Time
Warner? How much fairness could censorship proponents and their political leaders expect from Time and CNN, or from any journalist assigned to the story? No matter how ethical, scrupulous and professional
these journalists might be, their freedom from the appearance of conflict
of interest would be gone. How fair is that to citizens who expect and
depend on a free press to educate them on matters of public policy?

Once in my career I had to make a decision to put the *Chicago Tribune* in the Supreme Court on the side of *Hustler* magazine publisher
Larry Flynt in his First Amendment battle with the political preacher
Jerry Falwell. At stake was the right of a political cartoonist to satiri-
cally spear a public figure. The justification for siding with Flynt was
easy: If the Court ruled the wrong way, the government might be able
to outlaw a journalist's tool simply because it couldn't be kept out of
the pornographer's hand. The *Tribune* could support Flynt's case yet
stand apart from the rest of his work because there was no relationship,
financial or any other, between the *Tribune* and Hustler. In the public's
mind, one was journalism, the other entertainment. That distinction
was universally clear. Flynt was exploiting the integrity of journalism,
but we were never tarred with his brush.

Throughout our history, the free press has enjoyed a right to a special place in the democracy with special privileges under law because it was a special business with a unique goal of serving the public interest.

Journalism can't make that claim anymore. Except for a few newspaper companies, news organizations have become indistinguishable from other media. Journalists' pay checks come from the same payroll as those of the movie moguls, TV execs, radio personalities and record producers; from the same corporate bank accounts as the cash for independent movies and free-lance magazine pieces.

These same coffers are the source of virtually all the big book contracts that are handed out not to real authors but to tabloid journalists, kiss-and-tell gold diggers, toe-sucking, secret-spilling presidential political advisers and tattooed, rule-breaking, in-your-face athletes whose stock in trade is incivility.

The books are first promoted in the newspapers and on television and radio. Then they end up as movies—recycled "true story" programming with the same themes and audience appeal as the natural disasters, celebrity murders and presidential peccadilloes that are the perennial topics for the breathless television "journalistic" orgies.

The personalities involved cross the lines as easily as the subject matter. Radio's top money-maker, Rush Limbaugh, the voice of the Republican right, is newsmaker enough to guest on "Meet the Press" one month and entertainer enough to do the same on "The Drew Carey Show" the next. Morning talk sensation Howard Stern is a movie star, but so is Bernard Shaw and half the CNN news team, delivering fiction on the big screen in the same grim authoritative tones as they do real events.

How are we to tell the difference anymore?

In the last year, WMAQ-TV, NBC's Chicago affiliate, tried—unsuccessfully thank God—to make Jerry Springer, host of a sleazy daily talk show, a co-anchor of its nightly newscasts. And NBC's "Nightly News" gave special correspondent status to CNBC talk show host Geraldo Rivera, who long ago gave up his journalism credentials to host an embarrassing low-rent version of "Oprah." Reasons cited in both instances were the audience appeal and earning power of the two personalities.

A favorite phrase in the "lexicon" of the new entertainment/journalism—one often used by Geraldo himself—is "the smoking gun," meaning, of course, irrefutable evidence. For "the smoking gun" on what happened to the free press in America, look no further than its embarrassing performance on the most perfect of all television "news stories"—the Monica Lewinsky scandal. When two newspapers as serious and respected as *The Dallas Morning News* and *The Wall Street Journal* get so carried away with tabloidism that they both rush into print leaked phony stories using anonymous sources and then have to apologize, there's only one conclusion. With all due respect to my admired friend Harry Evans, it's past dusk. It is midnight in the garden and far too late to worry about fairness.

Jim Squires is a former political writer and editor of the Chicago Tribune *and onetime media advisor to Ross Perot. He is author of* Read All About It!: The Corporate Takeover of America's Newspapers.

15

Absolute Talk on the Radio

Ruth Bayard Smith

Looming over the interstates and secondary highways of metropolitan New York in the winter of 1998, the promotional billboards for WABC-AM—one of the premier talk radio stations in the country—were difficult to ignore. They featured huge photos of hosts Rush Limbaugh and Dr. Laura Schlessinger, and the imperative "Talk to Us."

On display for several months, they were a clear indicator that the landscape of American talk radio has evolved. Strongly associated with the conservative Limbaugh since he went on the air nationally in 1988, the medium has broadened its focus to embrace not just electoral issues, but the social and cultural questions that transcend public and private life.

Ratings released in March by the trade publication, *Talkers* magazine, show that the No. 1 place now belongs to no-nonsense tough-love advocate Dr. Laura Schlessinger, with 18 million listeners weekly. The No. 2 spot, with 17.5 million listeners, is held by "shock jock" Howard Stern. And the No. 3 position is Rush Limbaugh's, with an audience of 17.25 million.

At first glance, it may appear that political talk radio has been usurped by talk about relationships and preadolescent humor. However, a sense of absolutism and outrage still dominates the airwaves. For Rush Limbaugh, the issue is, of course, still conservative politics; for Howard Stern, it's fighting censorship; and for Dr. Laura Schlessinger, it's teaching moral values.

The similarities don't stop there. Each host feels he or she is providing an alternative to mainstream media; each has been received skeptically by articles in the press; and each has "high negatives," strong reactions from detractors who criticize them for ideology, for tone, for rhetorical style and for content.

And each has adoring loyal fans: Rush's Dittoheads, those callers who say "ditto" on the air to show their support for Limbaugh and his views; Howard Stern's followers who show up in droves when his books are published, impeding traffic in the process; and Dr. Laura's listeners who boast, "I am my kid's mom/dad," to show where their priorities lie.

With their quick repartee, lively manner and, yes, entertaining on-air approach, all three hosts understand the power of the medium. They recognize that many listeners experience radio as if the on-air personality were speaking directly to them. As a result, the hosts establish intimacy with their audience and with it authority. For all their topicality, their presentations have deep roots in the history of American politics and the history of the media.

Obviously, in America, presenting ideas in absolute terms—especially when insulting one's political opponents—is older than the country itself. And battles between the Federalists and anti-Federalists in the early days of the American republic were particularly vicious. In the 1920s and 1930s, when radio was a relatively new medium, the widely received broadcasts of Charles E. Coughlin, a radio priest, were notable first for their economic populism and later for their anti-Semitism.

A primitive form of talk radio began in the 1940s. Listeners would occasionally phone hosts, but limited telephone lines prevented the audience from hearing their remarks. More advanced technology allowed for actual phone-in talk radio in the late 1950s and early 1960s. Los Angeles' KABC-AM went all talk in 1960, with KMOX-AM in St. Louis, Mo., following soon after. Many stations adopted the format, at least for part of their schedule, and offered locally based programming on virtually everything from discussions of city government to entertainment interviews. Though some hosts like the late Joe Pyne told listeners with whom he disagreed "to gargle with razor blades," most programs were based on conversation rather than confrontation. However by the late 1970s, the FM band was attracting more and more listeners to its extensive musical selections, and AM talk radio was fading from earshot.

AM radio revived dramatically in the 1980s as a result of several factors: As part of a deregulation program at the FCC, the Fairness Doctrine was abolished, allowing stations to broadcast political material without having to present opposing points of view. At the same time satellite technology made it possible for programs to be syndicated cheaply around the country; no longer were talk programs focused only on local concerns. And with the proliferation of car phones, the reach of the medium seemed unstoppable.

The expanded medium was tailor-made for alienated voters, especially the so-called Reagan Democrats, who felt abandoned by their party. In fact, studies have shown that talk radio listeners actively follow the news and regularly vote. This aspect has not been lost over the years on local hosts who often marshaled the troops to support certain causes. For example, in the mid 1980s, Boston talkmeister Jerry Williams was largely credited with helping to repeal the Massachusetts seatbelt law (the law has since been reinstated). On a national level, even before the 1994 elections, radio talk programs were influential in stopping the congressional pay raises in 1989 and in vilifying George Bush over his tax hikes in 1990. President Clinton himself helped his election campaign in 1992 by schmoozing with Don Imus, and in early 1994 he phoned St. Louis' KMOX-AM radio from Air Force One to criticize Rush Limbaugh for some of his broadcasts. And in 1995, he denounced "the hate" heard on talk radio as a factor in the bombing of the federal building in Oklahoma City.

At the end of the 20th century, however, when the mainstream media is rife with stories of sexual misconduct, scandal and overall dysfunction, Stern, Limbaugh and Schlessinger make sense to listeners. What's more, they're not stuffy or inaccessible: They're presented as entertainment.

In fact, to tune in regularly to the programs of the top three hosts is to hear callers trying to make sense of a world they believe has gone amok. Their gratitude to be able to get on the air with someone who they believe "tells it like it is" is palpable; it's as if they have been given the opportunity to speak with the Oracle of Delphi.

Rush Hudson Limbaugh III has ruled the talk radio airwaves for the last 10 years. Largely credited with revitalizing AM radio, he moved to New York after a stint on a Sacramento, California, radio station, substituting for Morton Downey, Jr. Earlier he had worked in radio as a disc jockey under two different assumed names and with the Kansas City Royals in sales and special events.

Though Limbaugh takes a straight conservative line, the main focus of his broadcasts these days is President Clinton—the Whitewater investigation, the Paula Jones harassment suit, the Monica Lewinsky scandal (which he refers to as "tailgate") and whatever guests, speeches, events and press conferences are occupying the president's time. Other favorite topics are the media, illegal immigrants, environmentalists, Affirmative Action, liberals and feminists.

Limbaugh has always insisted that he doesn't set a national agenda as much as validate what people were already believing but weren't hearing or reading in the more mainstream media. The height of his reach was during the 1994 congressional elections when talk of Rush was ubiquitous. Newly elected Republicans made him an honorary member of their "class" and presented him with a plaque bearing the words "Rush was Right," acknowledging his role in getting them elected. In January 1995, a cover story in Time asked, "Is Rush Limbaugh good for America?"

Limbaugh's broadcasting formula has stayed constant over the years. With rare in-studio or on-the-phone interviews, the program, aired three hours daily from the headquarters of his Excellence in Broadcasting (EIB) Network in Manhattan, mixes humor and cutting commentary. Music plays an important part of the show, and Limbaugh often plays parodies of familiar tunes with cutting lyrics about liberals in general and President Clinton in particular. For instance, the recent "The Clintonian So-Slick Blues—Part II," sung to Bob Dylan's "Subterranean Homesick Blues," includes the line "Whitewatergate, Travelgate, Filegate, Funding-gate. Time to add the latest—Conjugate and Obfuscate." The Whitewater investigation had its own tune, the "Whitewater Debacle" sung to "Winchester Cathedral," as did Hillary Rodham Clinton with "The Little First Lady with Megalomania" based on "The Little Old Lady from Pasadena."

Both his books, *The Way Things Ought to Be* and *See, I Told You So* (which have set publishing records), expanded on what Limbaugh calls "Undeniable Truths of Life." Limbaugh published his first 35 Undeniable Truths in *The Sacramento Union* in 1988. Included in the list were such absolute statements as, "The greatest threat to humanity is the U.S.S.R."; "Abe Lincoln saved this nation"; "Feminism was established so as to allow unattractive women access to the mainstream of society"; and "The greatest football team in the history of civilization is the Pittsburgh Steelers of 1975-1980." An updated version, read on his program in February 1994, added that "evidence refutes liberalism"; "The only way liberals win national elections is by pretending they're not liberals"; "Ronald Reagan was the greatest president of the 20th century"; and "Too many Americans can't laugh at themselves anymore."

Howard Stern is commonly known as radio's "Bad Boy" because he pushes the envelope with his graphic sexual and scatalogical remarks.

However, more often than many critics will acknowledge, the focus of his program turns to the news and politics. Stern's sidekick Robin Quivers reads the news daily, playing straight woman to his commentary. Stern also endorses candidates and has featured New York-area politicians as his guests—particularly close to election time: Regulars have included New York Sen. Alphonse D'Amato, New York Gov. George Pataki and New Jersey Gov. Christine Todd Whitman. After her election in 1993, Whitman kept a campaign promise to name a highway rest stop after Stern. At a public press conference she acknowledged the reason: "He certainly went out of his way to endorse me during the campaign." Stern himself was bitten by the political bug when he ran briefly as the Libertarian candidate for governor of New York in 1994. (He withdrew when required to divulge his finances.)

Howard Stern has been relentless in his support of his right to say what he wants on the air, and as a result he and his employers have been repeatedly cited for obscenity. During a period when he was fined by the Federal Communications Commission for "indecency," he broadcast the following "prayer" about FCC Chairman Alfred Sikes: "Maybe the doctor will find more cancer in Sikes. That's the only thing I can pray for.... The only way I have a chance of ridding this guy out of my life is if people elect Bill Clinton, and we get rid of the religious.... I pray to you, Jesus, answer my prayers. Make their medical problems so bad that they cannot pay attention to me.... See, I don't pray to Jesus for stupid stuff like ratings. I pray for the important stuff like eliminating my enemies through cancer."

These statements are accepted by Stern's loyal listeners when they might not be from a different host, in part because they are caught up in the locker-room atmosphere of his broadcasts, syndicated nationally from New York's WXRK-FM (K-Rock). He is surrounded by a coterie of men who join him in relentlessly making coarse remarks, belching, passing gas and laughing. Occasionally Stern takes calls from people who phone to dispute something he's said. He will argue vociferously with them, ask them questions about their sex lives, their anatomy (women are often asked about the size of their breasts), and hang up and insult them.

Stern maintains that he's been successful because he developed a different kind of radio, though he eschews the title "shock jock." As he wrote in his book *Private Parts*, "I always resented the label of 'shock jock' that the press came up with for me, because I never intentionally set out to shock anybody. What I intentionally set out to do was to talk just as I talk off the air, to talk the way guys talk sitting around a bar."

Stern is the first to admit that he holds some very traditional views, many of them conservative: He's pro-capital punishment. He's outraged at much of society's behavior, especially towards children. And he's a family man with three daughters who are not allowed to listen to his program.

Today's No. 1 host, Dr. Laura Schlessinger betrays no interest in electoral politics, but she is unwavering in her preaching of morality and traditional values. Underlying each broadcast is the exhortation to "do the right thing," and she is unequivocal in her definition of what that is: no sex or "shacking up" before marriage, no day care and a return to old-fashioned mores and personal responsibility.

She began her career twenty years ago in Los Angeles by phoning Bill Ballance's controversial program "The Feminine Forum." He invited her back as his "human sexuality" expert, and within a year she had her own program in Orange County, Calif. For the last four years she's been syndicated nationally out of KFI-AM radio in L.A., and she's built her audience call by call and small market by small market.

For three hours each day she takes calls from listeners, mostly women, whose lives are seemingly on the edge and who have nowhere else to turn. They want to leave their husbands (not if there are children involved—unless there's abuse or infidelity, asserts Dr. Laura). They want to go back to work (nothing doing, says Dr. Laura, if the kids are of preschool age). They want their husbands to pay less attention to their ex-wives (too bad, Dr. Laura says, because their husbands chose to "make babies with them").

Schlessinger does not practice on-air therapy *per se*. She stops callers if she believes they're whining, blaming others for their troubles or speaking in psychobabble. Though she has had training in counseling and sex therapy, her Ph.D. is in physiology from Columbia University. She is deeply religious, and her program and her monthly newsletter are filled with references to her own recent conversion to Judaism and to others committed to religious precepts.

Her monologues and her conversations with callers are peppered with uncompromising terms such as "jerk," "slut," "bimbo" and "sperm donors"—a special phrase for irresponsible biological fathers. In September 1997, a column in New York magazine called her a "moral dominatrix."

Even the titles of her books go for the moral jugular: *How Could You*

Do That? The Abdication of Character, Courage, Conscience; Ten Stupid Things Women Do to Mess Up Their Lives; and the most recent *Ten Stupid Things Men Do to Mess Up Their Lives.*

It's estimated that about 70 percent of talk radio hosts nationally hold conservative views. There is a smattering of liberal and moderate hosts on commercial talk radio, but typically they too are paired with conservative counterparts. The result is often a shouting match, as exemplified by the team of Guardian Angels founder Curtis Sliwa and William Kunstler protégé Ron Kuby on WABC-AM in New York.

The argument that is often posited is that liberals just won't sell because they don't have what it takes to be provocative and entertaining. Even syndicated progressive host Ellen Ratner, president of the Washington-based Talk Radio News Service, says that liberals are simply "boring" and that she doesn't like to have them on her programs. At a forum at the Media Studies Center last April, former program director at WABC-AM radio John Mainelli conceded that he thought the liberal talk shows were "a little too Jerry Brown-like, a little too ponderous about the weight of the world on their shoulders."

Still, Rush Limbaugh, Howard Stern and Dr. Laura Schlessinger can be quite ponderous themselves: Their unwavering views of the world, while never dull, are delivered without a trace of doubt or questioning. And ultimately, for millions of listeners each week, those very qualities make them attractive.

Ruth Bayard Smith, a 1996–97 Media Studies Center fellow, is assistant professor of journalism at Montclair State University. She is writing "TALKTALKTALK: A History and Analysis of Talk Radio."

16

Looming Battles in Britain

Christopher T. Marsden

What guarantees the fairness of broadcast news—government regulation or a commercial marketplace of ideas? In the United States, the death of the Fairness Doctrine in 1987 ended four decades of regulation requiring broadcasters to address controversial public issues and cover them in ways that reflect contrasting viewpoints. Opponents of the Fairness Doctrine prevailed by arguing that it violated the First Amendment, that the marketplace provided a better guarantee of fairness than the Federal Communications Commission, and that the problem of spectrum scarcity, which limited the number of voices with access to the airwaves, had been removed by the widespread supply of local and national news through cable and satellite channels.

But in Britain, a country with a different broadcasting history and a different regulatory tradition, a battle over fairness regulation is looming in a media landscape defined by digitally converged media, consolidation of ownership and international broadcasting. At stake is not only a tradition of fairness bequeathed by the history of the British Broadcasting Corporation, but the very structure and rationales of British media regulations.

Britain has no First Amendment, no Bill of Rights and, at the moment, no written Constitution. Britons are subjects, not citizens, still granted no individual enforceable rights. In place of the legal protections afforded to Americans and most other developed nations, Britain has a system of discretion—meaning, in the case of broadcasting, broad powers given by statute for regulators to act upon. Out of this arrangement a classical tradition of "objectivity and impartiality" in news broadcasting has emerged.

This arrangement results from the insistence of the Independent Television Commission on "high quality" news programming. The United Kingdom's brand of fairness in the commercial television sector is provided through a mix of ITC Codes of Practice and a long tradition of excellence in broadcast journalism. This evolved due to one overriding factor: In contrast to American ideas of commercial competition in a marketplace (however tempered by the Fairness Doctrine in the period to 1987), in Britain excellent, and expensive, national and international news has always been supplied in a monopoly. ITV (Independent Television), the main commercial system, supports a news provider, ITN (Independent Television News), which supplies exclusive news to all three advertising-supported channels. ITN does not compete for funding with any other organization. The discretion to produce excellence was thus underwritten by virtually complete protection from market financial discipline, which prevented a "race to the bottom" in quality terms. Without the bean counters, journalists were free to pursue integrity and balance in a manner that their print journalist cousins could only envy.

Such fortuitous discretion was not confined to ITV; it stems from a tradition that the government first established in 1926. The BBC, cornerstone of British broadcast journalistic tradition and the model of broadcasting that Britain has exported around the world, has no formal independence from government. BBC is self-regulated by a board of governors, receives a royal charter and license to broadcast directly from the government of the day and is therefore reliant on government good favor for its continued existence. Fairness is an internal standard applied in a discretionary manner. All governors are government nominees; there are no parliamentary hearings to vet nominees. (This absolute discretion is shared with ITC commissioners. In fact, many BBC governors and even chairmen have also been ITC commissioners or chairmen.) A gilded circle of "the great and the good," as they are termed, which is more representative of the House of Lords than the people of Britain, has ruled benignly over broadcast regulation.

Proponents of digital convergence claim that this regulatory regime, designed to foster excellence and fairness, is both unsustainable and unnecessary. When digital television is launched, it will provide 20 or more new terrestrial channels and perhaps 500 satellite channels. Interactive electronic guides will enable Worldwide Web television and Intranet services, including home shopping and banking, through the main household television set. Competition in digital convergent media will provide a "'marketplace of ideas,'" in the classic 1919 statement of Oliver Wendell Holmes. Newspapers and television news will finally compete on equal terms for everything fit to Web cast.

Technological determinists claim that such bandwidth makes fairness provisions redundant, as newspapers can be accessed in the same way as broadcast services. Without monopoly rents to support their strengthened regulation, broadcasters should not be subjected to the unfair competition of fairness regulations. In Europe, where such concepts continue to be enshrined in the licensing of electronic media, such arguments are especially threatening to conventional journalism practices. According to the argument, the "media differences" concept, by which newspapers were subject to a lighter regulatory regime than analog television, is no longer sustainable. In Britain, the BBC will thus compete with the *Financial Times*, ITV with *The Sun* of London.

There are two fundamental difficulties with this economists' dream of a competitive environment. First, fairness regulations had little to do with spectrum scarcity and far more to do with the wilder excesses of the tabloids, which have grown far wilder since television removed any compunction to report serious news to the mass market. Radio and later television regulation was intended as a corrective on the excesses of the newspaper press. The predominant news source for the British populace is now the impartial television and radio news, rather than the tabloid press. Sexual morality plays comparable to the Clinton/Lewinsky affair are a weekly event in the pages of the best-selling U.K. newspaper, *The News of the World.*

The second problem for the convergent optimists is a residual skepticism in the United Kingdom that the promised proliferation of "channels" on the Internet will yield a meaningful alternative to the broadcast journalism tradition. Far more immediate is the dramatic reduction in media owners that accompanies the introduction of British digital television. In British television regulation, and in other countries following the British model, ownership pluralism accompanies editorial diversity and fairness. This combination of safeguards, jealously preserved by the commercial television regulator and the BBC board of governors throughout analog television history, was fatally undermined by the 1996 Broadcasting Act. ITV now has four major players, a radical departure from the 15 separate regional stations that operated freely in a federation until 1994. This concentration of ownership is defended as a response to the size of the U.S. market, to which British television continually suffers by export comparison. Unsurprisingly, ITN has suffered a dramatic squeeze on funding, staff levels and its high-quality news agenda as a result.

It would be excessive to describe a "tabloidization" of ITV's news provider, but excellence has clearly suffered due to competition. Fairness remains, but the "unwritten" contract by which monopoly players were granted *carte blanche* in the resources to invest in excellence has been eroded. With that will come an erosion in journalistic resources and, inevitably, standards.

Michael Green of Carlton, the largest of the new ITV combines, compares the history of U.K. regional ITV companies to "charming little thatched cottages in a landscape dominated by skyscrapers." Lobbying by Carlton and Granada, the other big player in ITV, led to their domination of the ITV system through a series of mergers in 1994 and 1997. The companies, in a "grand alliance" called British Digital Broadcasting, will control digital commercial television. If one believes the argument that "critical mass" in world markets is needed to compete with U.S. programmers, the logical answer supplied by government is that the old technological monopoly of analog broadcasters is replaced by a commercial digital monopoly of Carlton and Granada.

Spectrum scarcity may be reduced in the digital future, although the government does not expect the poorer segments of Britain to convert to digital terrestrial, let alone cable or satellite, before about 2009. British fairness regulations are likely to survive at least until then, under an informed bargain struck by the government with the BBC and ITN co-owners. News supply will come under continuing resource pressure, as a result of cost accounting within the new British skyscrapers. But the lofty heights that British broadcast news reporting occupied in the past will not be soon abandoned, at least in principle. Decades of ingrained editorial practice and executive discretion will not be replaced overnight, not least because the British approach is incrementalist, and journalistic commitment to fairness intense and durable. As a worst-case scenario, a subtler, more insidious coarsening is therefore more likely than a Big Bang.

The context of objectivity and impartiality will, however, change as British broadcast journalism becomes more of a global commodity. Although the BBC was widely seen to have blown its chance of global news programming in its failure to compete with CNN coverage of the Gulf War in 1991, that is now, belatedly, changing. The BBC has launched a 24-hour news channel, BBC24, on U.K. cable systems. The BBC has also launched a Web site and announced its intention of making BBC services, produced under British notions of fairness, available though all forms of delivery. If the BBC is to export its news globally, in competition with the free-market product of Fox News, MSNBC and CNN, it will need carriage on computer networks in the convergent future. Satellite and cable networks may result in a "Marketplace of Ideas Everywhere"; the BBC can only compete if it marries its content to operating systems run by potential rivals such as Microsoft, to accompany "Windows Everywhere."

All this may mean a shift in doctrines of fairness, not their abandonment. If international viewers in the digital future are to find a balanced view of Iraq, they will require more than British compromises that keep broadcast journalism traditions alive. The need for fairness concerns may extend from news reporting itself to the gatekeeping role of computer, telco, cable and programming supply. Broadcast regulators are having to become specialized antitrust regulators.

Older notions of the proper road to fairness, grounded in state regulation, are everywhere exposed to the commercial marketplace of ideas. Which will citizens embrace? The battle may be lost in the States; it is warming up nicely to the Communications Bill 2000 in Britain.

Christopher T. Marsden is director of the European Media Regulation Group at the School of Law, University of Warwick, England.

17

What Price Fairness?

Monroe E. Price

A 1998 ruling of the Independent Television Commission's impos-
ing hefty fines on the broadcaster MED-TV illustrates the special complexities and idiosyncracies of applying British notions of fair broadcasting in an increasingly global world.

MED-TV, which has little audience in the United Kingdom, was
established in London to distribute programming via satellite to Kurds
around the world. It especially sought to reach Kurdish minorities in
Turkey, Iran and Iraq. Its programming, produced largely in Belgium,
is a mix of news, entertainment and education. MED-TV programming
seems to be hugely important to a historically diasporic community of
35 million Kurds that is trying to rediscover and redefine its nation-
hood and reaffirm its language and culture.

But Turkey, engaged in an armed conflcit with Kurdish separatists,
views MED-TV as virtually the media arm of the PKK (Kurdistan
Workers Party), the separatist Kurdish force that has been fighting Turkish troops. Turkish leaders deem the PKK a terrorist organization and a
significant threat to the integrity and indivisibility of Turkey.

Turkish officials have pressured the British government, because MED-
TV was licensed in London, to withdraw MED-TV's license and close
down the bustling producer. They claim that MED-TV is a "political
organization" and therefore precluded from obtaining a British broadcasting license. Turkey has also pressured governments of nations such
as Belgium to deny MED-TV satellite transponder space and has encouraged police searches and seizures at its production facilities.

In February 1998 the ITC, the public body responsible for regulat-
ing and licensing British commercial television, penalized MED-TV

for three broadcasts to the tune of a total of 90,000 pounds ($144,000)—
a large fine, by the standards of ITC. According to the Commission,
despite formal warnings, MED-TV violated the impartiality requirements of ITC's programming code.

In one breach, said the ITC, a "40 minute long programme consisted
entirely of a political rally organised by the PKK." The violation: "No
context was supplied and there was no balancing material." In a second
breach of impartiality requirements, MED-TV "seemingly endorsed" a
condemnation of a U.S. list of terrorist organizations that included
certain Kurdish groups. In a third transgression of the ITC's rules on
the neutrality of journalists, a fine was imposed for "personal comments" after a MED-TV journalist in the field described members of
the relatively moderate Kurdish Democratic Party as "treacherous and
murderous."

MED-TV is paying its fines in installments.

*Monroe E. Price, a 1998 Center fellow, is professor of law at Yeshiva
University's Cardozo Law School.*

Part 3

Fairness—A Goal

18

What Makes a Journalist Fair?

Rep. Lee H. Hamilton

I am impressed by how many of my Indiana constituents view the news media with suspicion. Many of them wonder whether they can really believe what they read and hear, and ask the fundamental question, "How can we know the truth?"

American journalists have long had a reputation for independence and integrity combined with hard-nosed reporting and sharp investigative skills. Americans have traditionally looked to journalists to get basic, factual information on national events. The news media often put the spotlight on difficult problems and can be an important force for understanding and change. At its best, American journalism can be very good indeed.

But as I look at coverage of Congress and government today, I am troubled by many of the trends I see. First, I am quite alarmed that the cynicism with which many journalists seem to view public officials creeps into reporting. Coverage is dominated by the problems and scandals of government, like government waste and corruption, with very little attention to the successes of government—like the creation of the Internet, the vast improvement in older Americans' health as a result of Medicare or breakthroughs in medical research.

Second, important national issues sometimes receive only cursory coverage, without the level of detail or depth the public and policymakers need to make good decisions. Conversely, sometimes relatively minor issues receive disproportionate coverage. I am concerned that the news media are reducing their coverage of government and foreign policy and increasing their coverage of entertainment personalities and human-interest stories.

Third, journalists too often blend fact and commentary.

Fourth, the news media sometimes don't present clearly and fairly the best arguments on all sides of an issue. Too often the story is either tilted toward one particular point of view, factually incorrect, or the focus of the story is on the politics of the issue rather than the policy debate.

The result is that the public is confused about where the truth lies, skeptical about the accuracy and completeness of the news they are given and doubtful about the ability of government to accomplish anything important. More and more my constituents are relying on nontraditional sources, such as special-interest publications, to get information. They simply don't trust the national news media anymore to give them basic facts or unbiased reporting.

I am especially concerned about these trends because of the essential role of the press in the relationship between citizens and elected officials. In our political system, we rely on the press to inform citizens about government actions and policy debates, to help public officials gauge public opinion and to act as a watchdog. By deciding whether and how extensively events or issues are covered, the press influences the policy agenda.

One of the major changes I have seen in American politics during my career has been the erosion of public trust in government. In the mid 1960s, three quarters of Americans said they trusted the federal government to do the right thing most of the time. In recent years, that number has generally been closer to one third. This devaluation of government and politics makes it all the more difficult for the federal government to carry out its important responsibilities as we enter the 21st century.

There are many reasons for this drop in trust, of course, and several of them can be addressed by political leaders. For example, balancing the budget to strengthen the economy has improved public confidence in government. But there is a clear relationship between the public's confidence in the news media and its confidence in the government. In a recent major Harvard study, the increasingly negative, cynical tone of coverage of government was found to be one of the biggest factors in this decline in public confidence. And that is not a problem that policymakers can or should solve; it's one that the news media will have to change from within.

The best journalists balance a healthy skepticism with a basic respect for people and for the political process. Journalists ought to ask difficult questions of public officials. They ought to look at how we run our campaigns and our offices. They ought to give careful examination to our views and the policy solutions we advocate. And they ought to ask whether there are important issues that government is failing to address, and if so, why. All of these questions foster accountability and transparency in our democracy.

Whether they ask these questions in a combative or dispassionate manner is not really all that important. What is important is whether they listen to the answers. My concern is that too often, skepticism becomes cynicism in the mind of the journalist. Skeptics come to an interview prepared to ask tough questions, but also to consider the responses. Cynics believe they know the answers to the questions before they ask them. Their premise is that the public official is lying. I know too many reporters who seem to think that all politicians are on the take, that we are without fail motivated only by self-interest and never by the common good, that we really don't care much about what our constituents want. Certainly there are inept and corrupt politicians, but there are fortunately many others who are dedicated public servants. The best reporters view politicians as neither inherently dishonest nor inherently virtuous.

In addition, the best journalists are driven by genuine curiosity. They take the time to develop a deep understanding of the issues they cover. I have been fortunate to know a number of journalists who have an impressive expertise in foreign policy or economics, for example. But I have also encountered many who come to an interview just to get a quote, without a thorough enough understanding to really delve into the issues. Sometimes this is understandable: The number of issues facing Congress in any given year is vast, and reporters cannot be an expert on each one.

Fortunately, the competitive instinct among journalists is very strong. That sometimes leads to excess and inaccuracies, but also contributes to a corrective process: If one news outlet reports a story badly, other rival organizations will try to set the record straight.

Not all policy issues are exactly scintillating, of course. One journalist who had covered Congress for many years called my office while writing a story on an appropriations bill and said to me, "You know, a lot of the work that Congress does is just plain boring." That may be true, but journalism does the public a disservice if it simply ignores policy in favor of an emphasis on horse-race politics. Part of journalism's mission in this country is to try to provide a common ground of knowledge and analysis, to clarify the national debate and link it to people and their lives. Too often the news media suggest that politics is little more than the struggle for power between ambitious politicians and has less to do with how we as a country deal with the serious problems confronting us.

In my view, the ideal is the independent, nonpartisan, nonideological journalist who does everything possible to filter out of reporting his or her personal political views. Journalists are, of course, going to have opinions about the issues and people they cover. It is foolish to pretend otherwise. But to the extent possible, they should try to set those opinions aside and not allow them to imbue their reporting.

Good journalists realize that their job is to report on policy and politics, not to participate in them. It seems to me today that too many journalists, especially those based in Washington, want to be policy players rather than reporters of events. They want to give advice to the public and to prominent politicians, to score political points rather than illuminate events and to make themselves into media celebrities. We see this trend perhaps most clearly on political talk shows, some of which are little more than shouting matches. They do not analyze, explain or clarify the issues facing the country.

Despite its flaws, I favor a powerful press because it can balance the power of government. I may complain about journalists on occasion, but I know I would not like the country without them. Their job is formidable. We should not resent but applaud the efforts reporters make to investigate and to keep the record straight. The news media have an obligation to ferret out scandal. They have the obligation to cover contests for public office. Because the news media have a high mission in a democratic society, they must be all the more responsible in carrying it out.

When I first came to Washington many years ago, a journalist told me to take the time occasionally to put my feet on the desk, look out the window and think about the country and its problems. That's good advice for politicians and good advice for journalists too. If it were more widely heeded, I think we would see greater attention to the vitally important issues on the public agenda, more thorough and balanced coverage of them and a fairer assessment of the achievements and shortcomings of government and public officials.

While I am sometimes dismayed by the trends I see in journalism today, I have had the opportunity during my career in public service to interact with many talented, dedicated journalists. And I can count relatively few times in my many years in office that I have read or heard a news story that I thought was grossly inaccurate or unfair to me. The majority of the journalists I deal with genuinely want to get the story right and work hard to do so.

Rep. Lee H. Hamilton of Indiana has served thirty-four years in the House of Representatives. He is ranking Democrat on the House International Relations Committee.

19

All Is Not Fair in Journalism

Carlin Romano

Imagine a group of beltway insiders coming together one Saturday morning to be fair to one another. (I did say *imagine*). To guarantee the justice of the procedure, they're relieved of their memories as they enter the Georgetown mansion selected for the experiment.

Suddenly no participant can recall whether he or she is ABC's White House correspondent, a deputy assistant to the president, an aide to Sen. Trent Lott, a Ken Starr staffer, a network news president or even Matt Drudge (in town for the weekend). Stripped of all knowledge of their status in Washington society, not to mention the tastes, values and ideologies that got them there, they're primed to act without bias.

The task amid this calculated amnesia is to debate and choose the principles by which Washington—a society fueled by powerful political, journalistic and governmental institutions—will fairly distribute its appropriate benefits and burdens: power, publicity, scoops, money, White House invitations, Sunday talk-show gigs.

Philosophy types will recognize the scenario as suspiciously like the "original position," conducted behind a "veil of ignorance," that Harvard philosopher John Rawls famously posited twenty-five years ago as a thought experiment to test our intuitions about justice. The instinct behind Rawls' hypothetical rings true to many: Given the powerful hold that self-interest exerts on us, fairness can only emerge from a scenario in which no one knows how the rules chosen will affect his self-interest. To Rawls in his now classic A *Theory of Justice* (1973) and subsequent work, fairness is the core of justice because fairness typically applies to procedures and institutions, while "justice" is the word we use to categorize outcomes. (Justice Frankfurter's famous remark that "the history of American freedom is, in no small measure, the history of procedure" suggests the same weighting.) In Rawls' model, a key principle of justice chosen is the so-called difference principle, according to which "the least advantaged members of society" should gain from any unequal distribution of goods.

One can imagine various responses from the Beltway mediocracy. Tabloid types might divide into those offering a simple "Huh?" and those slightly more able to follow the inference: "Uh, does that mean some intern has to get a better job, no matter how we structure things?"

Better-educated broadsheet and talking-head types might tear their hair out at the thought of giving up hard-won name recognition even for a morning, regardless of the chance to participate in a kind of Constitutional Convention on Fairness. Or they might rise to the exercise. The amnesiac journalists might agree to rules that require the press to undertake "environmental damage" assessments on future stories. Politicians and officials could grasp the virtue of doling out accurate information immediately rather than slowly and resentfully. We might just get a "fairer" system of journalism.

If you haven't seen the Rawls model come up recently on the Sunday blabfests, or in another blatantly anti-Clinton story for the *New York Post* by Deborah Orin, it's no mystery. What journalists consider fair—or fair-minded—and what philosophers think about the topic, is so galactically distant from each other as to require NASA-enhanced communication between parties.

Journalists, like most nonphilosophers, tend to equate "fairness" with any established procedure that's not under immediate challenge from a powerful interest group and causes no obvious, direct harm to others.

Philosophers think it's a mite more complicated.

Philosophers think of fairness as involving notions such as justice, equality, proportionality, reciprocity and impartiality, regardless of whether they accept Rawls' version. They're sensitive to how any maxim of action purporting to be fair and potentially universal (e.g., Break any good story you get, regardless of the consequences.) should be tested by a universally applicable golden rule (Would you accept it as a maxim governing the action of others toward you?). They recognize that the word "fairness" has a history, that it metaphorically connotes following a straight route. As the philosopher A. John Simmons has noted, "The moral meaning of fairness is at least loosely connected with the nonmoral meanings of the term: straightness, beauty, flawlessness, proper proportion (as in 'fair weather,' 'fair of face,' 'fair ball')."

Philosophers think of fairness as primarily a feature of rules attached to procedures and institutions in which a variety of people cooperate to achieve a common good. That would make the natural way to ask the question about what's been going on in American journalism lately, "Is the *system* of media coverage fair?"

Of course, that's not the way the press asks the question. It asks, "Is the press fair? or "Are the media fair?" as if the obligations and duties of one segment of the media system could be addressed in isolation.

The model is Darwinian, not Rawlsian. Individualist, not communitarian. Selfish, some might say, rather than kindly.

You see the problem.

So asking a philosopher to advise a 1990s journalist on what counts as "fair-mindedness" runs into an immediate roadblock—call it journalism's "fairness gap." By the standards of philosophers, it's not that journalists occasionally act unfairly. It's that fairness, properly understood, is not a part of their rational calculations at all.

Discussing one of several putative stories about Clinton being caught in a compromising position with Lewinsky, *New York Times* managing editor Bill Keller told *Editor & Publisher*: "A lot of other people have just picked up the story and attributed it to ABC. The stampeding herd has gotten so big and so ferocious that it requires a lot more backbone to stand up in a case like this."

A much-respected Pulitzer-Prize-winning foreign correspondent, Keller offered *E&P* a remarkably candid assessment of the hard calls he'd been facing every day, trying to put out a newspaper committed to high standards of fairness.

"There isn't a clear-cut formula. It's a gut judgment."

Imagine someone asking John Rawls, newly named managing editor of the *Times*, how he would run the paper (which inevitably allocates benefits and burdens) to ensure that it operated fairly.

"There is a clear-cut formula. You need to get as many of the people affected by the paper's activity as possible together in a very large room. As they enter, you use that zap gun from *Men in Black* to selectively destroy their memories. Then you begin the process of deliberation. It's not a gut judgment."

Rawls would need an intellectual makeover as drastic as Drudge's fashion fix-up for his "Meet the Press" debut. Until he got it, Rawls would be running *The New York Behind-the-Times*.

Keller's honest admission reflects the reality of the news business and why philosophical notions of fairness seem so remote. Yet it would be utterly *unfair* and flat wrong to suggest that principled journalists like Keller are not trying to be fair in their decisions. Are philosophers and journalists simply caught in a paradox when it comes to fairness?

Not quite. You might describe things this way. American journalists see themselves as operating in a governmental and social system, ordered and sanctified by the First Amendment, in which the fundamental principles of fairness, as well as pressures *for* fairness, have already been established. Within that system, they're free to think *instrumentally* rather than *philosophically*. The goal is to get the news, to get the truth, and get it right. The consequences will play out however they play out. The job is mechanical—getting and supplying information. Other principles and pressures—libel law, the First Amendment, competition, media criticism, reader attitudes—will nudge the operation into some semblance of fairness. In any event, the chief sense of fairness is fairness *in regard to the truth*.

Philosophers, though, can't accept that. If anything distinguishes philosophical thought from journalistic thought, it's the inability of the former to cop out on a complete articulation of its position on a subject, from fundamental principles to practical upshots (Hell, that's pretty much the job description!). Philosophers therefore recognize, to highlight one point, that truth is not the sort of entity to which fairness is owed. Fairness is owed to people (and, Kant would argue, all rational sentient beings).

To the philosopher, therefore, anything short of synoptic, systematic thinking about fairness to other people—by every reporter, editor and producer on a daily basis—must fall short of fair-mindedness. Occasionally, in newsrooms, journalism schools and think tanks, journalists recognize the force of the synoptic argument—they feel the fairness gap. They exchange views on whether the photographer should photograph the baby thrown from a building or try to catch it. They argue over whether the foreign correspondent should intervene to save a refugee's life or just report what happens. Most of the time, though, they're too busy to think such questions through.

This seems a lugubrious conclusion. Must we then place the ideal of truly fair-minded journalism, *philosophically* fair-minded journalism, in the dustbin of crackpot Utopian notions? Plainly, most journalists would say no. They'd make all sorts of trench-level recommendations about what would constitute fair-minded journalism today. Watching out for ax-grinding among sources. Giving any person attacked a chance to answer back. And so on.

From a philosopher's viewpoint, those recommendations, while welcome, would simply enhance fairness to *truth* (which doubtless provides some derivative forms of fairness to people) without directly enhancing fairness to *people*. All the efforts in the world to make sure that reporting on Clinton's sex life is accurate would not address whether it is *fair* to Clinton—the human being—to report on his sex life, or fair to his wife, or fair to readers to impose such coverage on them—in their interest, of course—even when they say they don't want it.

A philosopher, in contrast, might want to make the following suggestion, even if it did not turn a generation of Matt Drudges into a herd of John Rawls thinkalikes. The fundamental recommendation—make that requirement—for journalists to be fair-minded is simple.

In deciding how to act on a day-to-day basis, they must not only take into account the interests of everybody else involved in the news process, but *act according to whatever rules they think will most fairly distribute benefits and burdens among those people*. They need to do that even if they're too egotistical to shed their identities at someone's door, too busy to try the Rawlsian experiment on a Saturday (Hey, that's speaking-engagement day!) and too worried that participation will draw the awful and demeaning mockery that Hillary Clinton suffered after her philosopher-induced "conversations" with Eleanor Roosevelt.

On this model, Mike McCurry needs to think if he's being fair to Ken Starr and Sam Donaldson. Ken Starr needs to think if he's being fair to Ms. Lewinsky. Deborah Orin needs to think if she's being fair to all those journalism students who might be reading her. Linda Tripp needs to think....

Would we have a better news system? The philosopher in me likes the idea. The reporter in me has no damn idea how I'm going to find the time.

You see the problem.

Carlin Romano, a 1988–89 Media Studies Center fellow and literary critic of The Philadelphia Inquirer, *has taught philosophy at Yale University, the University of Pennsylvania and Bennington College.*

20

Divided People, Divided Press

John O'Farrell

In northern Ireland, to use the internationally accepted name for the place of which I write, it is generally assumed that journalists take sides. The place name you use spells out your allegiance: "The North of Ireland," or just "Ireland," is commonly used by Irish nationalists or republicans who want to see the entire island consolidated into the Irish republic. "Ulster" is used by unionists or loyalists who favor the link with Britain. "Northern Ireland" itself is favored by British commentators and politicians, while "The North" is the most commonly used term in the Republic of Ireland. More hard-line republicans call it "Occupied North-East Ireland," while loyalists reciprocate by referring to the Republic of Ireland ("The South" to northern nationalists) as "*Eire*," a name officially dropped in 1949. Which province do you want to live in?

We in Northern Ireland are a divided people. If the press reflects the society it reports, how do these divisions—cultural, social, religious, political, even ethnic—manifest themselves in reporting? Does a sectarian society necessarily have to have a sectarian press? If everyone is biased, is there an ideological center that can act as a fulcrum for a definition of fairness? Alternately, how far can bias go? Is it limited by the realization that the discrediting and destruction of an enemy may rebound? Is reporting of the peace process subject to self-censorship in order to maintain the process itself?

The media that report on Northern Ireland can be divided into two groups: print and broadcast media within Northern Ireland, and print and broadcast media that serve news organizations based outside Northern Ireland. These two groups operate, it can be argued, by different standards of "fairness," based on their audience and governmental restrictions. For example, in the city of Belfast, there are three daily news-papers: the *News Letter*, the *Irish News* and *the Belfast Telegraph*. The *News Letter*, the oldest continuously printed English-language news-paper on Earth, takes a unionist viewpoint, between the right wing of the Ulster Unionist Party and Ian Paisley's Democratic Unionists. It is contemptuous of loyalist paramilitaries, but its real spleen is directed at Irish nationalism in general and what it calls "Sinn Féin/IRA" in particular. It uses a house style that insists in calling the Republic *"Eire,"* and its *taoiseach* the "Irish prime minister," emphasizing the foreignness of its island neighbor. The *Irish News* takes a nonviolent nationalist viewpoint; it is critical of IRA violence but tends to blame the unionists and the British for the woes of "The North." The *Telegraph* is an evening paper that takes a liberal unionist viewpoint but allows regular opinion pieces from all political viewpoints, from loyalist to republican.

Northern Ireland is unusually well served by a number of local weekly newspapers supported by a loyal readership of between 10,000 to 25,000. Most decent-sized towns have at least two newspapers, whose views reflect their readership. Dungannon, a market town in County Tyrone with a roughly 50–50 unionist/nationalist population, has both a union-ist and a nationalist newspaper. Larne, a staunchly unionist town, has two newspapers reflecting the two main strands of unionism—the Ul-ster Unionists and Democratic Unionists. These newspapers do not at-tempt to educate or alter the perceptions of their readers, rather they reflect their views (or prejudices).

Marshall McLuhan's aphorism about people not reading their paper but sinking into it like a warm bath is appropriate here. Broadcast me-dia is shackled by the legal requirements to achieve "balance"—as de-fined by the codes of practice of the British Broadcasting Corporation and the Independent Broadcasting Authority—and therefore outrages political operators of all hues. Nationalists accuse the BBC in particu-lar of being run by a Masonic cabal that tends towards an Anglocentric viewpoint, while unionists point accusingly at journalists with "Irish" names (such as *Séamus* or *Mairéad*). Political parties with paramilitary connections point to a culture of self-censorship, replacing the statu-tory censorship that banned Sinn Féin, the Progressive Unionists and Ulster Democrats from the airways from 1988 until 1994. The recent inclusion of these three parties into acceptable political debate on radio and television has been important for those parties obviously, but also for the wider audience, who tended to demonize them as terrorist apolo-gists. It has also been important for journalists, who could not easily dismiss the views of these parties, particularly as recent elections have shown more than 20 percent combined support for SF, the PUP and UDP, larger than the center vote, which averages 15 percent of the electorate.

When we turn to journalists who report for media organizations based outside Northern Ireland, different rules and agendas come into play. One of the reasons that "the Troubles" has had a wide international audience, and therefore the consequent reason that people here have an inflated impression of the importance of our angst, is that we are white and speak English. There are 1.5 million people involved. There have been just over 3,000 fatalities. Over 29 years. That's peanuts. There are 100 violent conflicts on the boil in the New World Order. Algeria, Kosovo, Rwanda, Chiapas, East Timor or Kurdistan make us look like amateurs, with casualty lists that drown our real tragedies with the tears of millions. Northern Ireland is an important story. Its resolution will be a sign, and not just to the people living here, that the demons of ethnic nationalism can be overcome, that the reason of the Enlightenment will prevail over the superstitious sectarianism of the Reformation and the Counter-Reformation. We can worry about postmodernism later.

Reporters for news organizations based outside Northern Ireland see themselves as uniquely impartial; as "outsiders" they are somehow above the fray. While their reporting is generally balanced, the editorial lines of their newspapers are anything but. With the exception of the *Daily Mirror*, whose "Troops Out" line has been blunted over recent years, every London paper has always adopted a prounion stance. The Republic's papers, with the exception of the *Sunday Independent*, take a "soft" nationalist line—somewhere between John Hume's Social Democratic and Labor Party and the Irish government—which holds that Irish unity can only happen with unionist consent.

It could be argued that the editorial lines of papers in London and Dublin are at least subconsciously affected by the political moods around them. Policies of bipartisanship have operated in both capitals for the past 30 years, producing a self-conscious consensus that has deepened over the past five years as Irish "soft" nationalism and British "soft" unionism have politically merged.

The consequence is a severe disincentive to rock the boat. Questioning the peace process or its players invites accusations that one prefers a state of war. Questioning the pervasive and intrusive security state that still exists in Northern Ireland invites accusations that one is "soft" on terrorism. Indeed, distancing oneself from "terrorism" is a popular field sport. It means the bizarre spectacle of "democratic" politicians queuing up to "condemn" the latest atrocity while challenging other politicians to do likewise in a unique ritual of the virility of their constitutionality. Those who do not condemn, meaning those whose paramilitary friends have done the dirty deed, are themselves condemned for not condemning, and so it goes.

At this stage, I should bring myself into the frame, just so my apparent bias is clear. I was born in Dublin, where I lived until four years ago. A planned stay in Belfast has become permanent, for personal as much as professional reasons. Three years ago, I became managing editor of *Fortnight*, a small independent current affairs and arts magazine founded in 1970. *Fortnight* was specifically started as a response to the Troubles and a reaction to the sectarian basis of print media in Northern Ireland.

Fortnight has a policy of encouraging debate by publishing the views of all political persuasions, which naturally causes reactions. It is a point of perverse pride that the magazine has been accused of being pawns of the IRA, Ulster Volunteer Force, the Alliance Party, SDLP and British Intelligence. On the big constitutional issues, it strives toward neutrality, but on social, economic and cultural issues, it is unashamedly liberal. This means arguing for unpopular measures, such as gay rights and the extension of the abortion laws that prevail in the rest of the United Kingdom but are vetoed here by the fundamentalist Catholic and Protestant supporters of the SDLP and unionist parties.

The fact is, however, that *Fortnight* faces justified charges that it is as ghettoized as the nationalist *Irish News* or the unionist *News Letter*; its readers and contributors tend to be from a small left/liberal clique. Another unfortunate, but valid, perception is that *Fortnight* is geographically limited: People in Britain think it is Irish; Irish people in the Republic think it is northern; Northern Ireland people from rural areas or Derry think it is too Belfast; most of Belfast associate it with the square mile around Queen's University, a psychological ghetto of self-conscious liberalism.

Nevertheless, this low-circulation (4,000) journal of the native "cultural elite" has some clout among the local political class. Editing *Fortnight* has afforded me unique access to both the workings of power and the politics of the paramilitaries. The reactions I get from people are interesting: As a southerner, am I therefore a nationalist? As editor of *Fortnight*, am I a liberal? As a middle-class (nonpracticing) Roman Catholic, is my natural political home the SDLP or the Alliance Party?

As a socialist, do I favor Sinn Féin or the Progressive Unionists or the British Labor government? For what it's worth, I choose not to exercise my franchise here. I believe that I have a duty to my readers to strive for as little partiality as possible; therefore I cop out of making the necessary subjective choices one has to make when one contemplates voting. Furthermore, the more I learn about the people and parties that offer themselves for election, the less I want to vote for any of them.

The SDLP epitomizes the middle-class Catholic chauvinism I grew up hating in the Republic. The Ulster Unionists combine a smug "born to rule" attitude with frightening sectarianism, institutionalized through their constitutional link with the Orange Order. The Democratic Unionists are a crypto-fascist mélange of flat-earthers and cynical sectarian manipulators. Sinn Féin spout dreams of an Irish socialist utopia but exert control of their ghetto strongholds through blackballing opponents and punishment beatings. The two loyalist parties are wannabe Sinn Féins for poor Protestants. Alliance think the world owes them a living for not being as hate-ridden as the other parties. A plaque on all their houses. There are individuals within these parties who are heroically trying to alter the sclerosis that has afflicted the North's political parties, but those few good men and women tend to hide behind party lines when the going gets tough.

It follows that the people most disappointed by my journalism are those who presume that I owe them some allegiance. (Not that John Hume or I lose sleep about that.) The fact is that whenever a politician opens his mouth into a passing microphone, no matter if it's in South Africa or South Armagh, the primary audience for his remarks are his (and it is almost always his) immediate supporters. Such is the parochial (not to say patriarchal) nature of politics in Northern Ireland that it is very difficult to get politicians to go on the record with any original thoughts.

The field is left to barren sectarian clichés, where "our" side is always the innocent victim of "their" crimes. Therefore unionist spokesmen can overlook half a century of abusive rule under the effective one-party state that was the Stormont government, scrapped by the British in 1972, and point at the crimes of the IRA over three decades as the beginning and end of all of our problems. The IRA justify their crimes as a reaction to Stormont, the Royal Ulster Constabulary or 800 years of British involvement in Ireland. Loyalist paramilitaries claim their sectarian murders of Catholics are provoked by the IRA. Both the British and Irish governments wash their hands of any responsibilities, propagating the fiction that they are honest brokers in a religious-based tribal conflict, a polite fiction whereby they depoliticize the situation, absolve themselves of blame for the political vacuum that encourages demagogues and situate themselves above the squabbling tribes.

A problem with the "two tribes" analysis is that it ignores the real debate that happens continually within, as much as between, the six or seven unionist parties and the five or six nationalist political groupings. A real brain drain has occurred, with the middle classes, business, trade unions and agricultural interests evacuating the field. The character of those attracted to politics tends towards the maverick. While "maverick" is usually a complimentary description in our individualist Western culture, the Northern Irish maverick tends towards the power hungry and ruthless end of the definition. We get the sort of man who is bursting with frustration until some level of power is reached within his party, permanently watching his back as he sharpens his knife, eyes fixed on the space between the shoulder blades of the party colleague ahead of him.

Journalists in Northern Ireland have to bear this in mind every time they get an interview or briefing from a politician here. The chances of one risking his career by sounding too magnanimous to the other side, and therefore selling out his own party or people are minimal. Everyone remembers the lesson of Bill Craig, the fastest rising star of the hard unionist right in the early 1970s until he thought twice about the violent consequences of his rhetoric and actions. When he proposed a voluntary coalition between the unionists and the constitutional nationalism of the SDLP, he fell victim to the same unionist backlash that supported him: his Westminster seat was taken by his former deputy, and he sank into obscurity and alcoholism. Among current unionist leadership, David Trimble is savagely criticized from both within his Ulster Unionists party and the second largest unionist party, the Democratic Unionists, for his participation in peace talks.

Similarly, Sinn Féin's Gerry Adams faces accusations within the republican movement, publicly from the sister of Bobby Sands, whose death on hunger strike in 1981 elevated him to the status of the movement's most potent martyr, and privately from dissident IRA men exploding bombs and shooting people.

In the final hours of the Easter 1998 negotiations in Stormont, as the British and Irish prime ministers worked for three days to reach an agreement acceptable to both sides, the spin operation from the parties and governments was extraordinary. The story shifted every two hours in a political tennis match. Reporters conveyed news to the newsmakers: For the parties in the talks, hourly bulletins and regular phone calls from journalists were the main way of learning what "the other side" was saying.

It was a concentrated version of an old pattern in Northern Ireland that is likely to persist into the future. Politicians feed stories to journalists with an eye to how the news will play to both their own side and their adversaries. The "other side" interprets the news according to the veracity of the story, the source, the journalist and their news organization. The result is a process of communication that is intense yet wary and indirect.

This has to be borne in mind while interviewing politicians. On the record, one gets platitudes and clichés. Off the record, one can either hear unprintable sectarian bile, or well-thought-out ideas on the future. Politicians take into account the track record of the reporter and her/his media organization. Previous bad press is long remembered. To give a personal example, UUP leader David Trimble will have nothing to do with *Fortnight* due to a disagreement with a previous editor.

My Dublin accent precludes me from safely entering loyalist areas in Belfast, where I may be seen as a hostile interloper. The telephone is much safer.

Resistance and mistrust that confront *Fortnight* have been overcome by invitations to write op-ed pieces, which we run unaltered, bearing only libel in mind. News judgments have consequences too. We thought long and hard before publishing evidence that the IRA were breaking their 1994–96 cease-fire by shooting alleged drug dealers, using the cover name Direct Action Against Drugs. A local tabloid newspaper had evidence that a prominent party leader had engaged in a string of adulterous affairs, but it succumbed to pressure from the two governments as well as the individual concerned and killed the story on the basis that it would undermine the peace talks.

People are wary whether a settlement can be reached, let alone work. That doesn't stop people from hoping that it will work. In Northern Ireland pessimism of the intellect battles optimism of the spirit; journalists do not stand apart from this fight. Indeed, with all its problems and frustrations, many better journalists than I think Northern Ireland is the most interesting story around. I daily pay private tribute to the inspiring brilliance of people like David McKitterick of *The Independent* of London, Mary Holland of *The Observer*, Peter Taylor of the BBC, Kevin Cullen of *The Boston Globe*, David Sharrock of *The Guard-*

ian, David Dunseath of BBC Radio Ulster, Deaglán De Bradún of *The Irish Times* and Eamonn McCann, Susan McKay and Ed Maloney of Dublin's *Sunday Tribune*.

Yet in covering Northern Ireland, journalists face painful dilemmas. Imagine yourself a reporter who possesses facts that, if published, could undermine politicians who might make a historic compromise with sworn enemies. Do you publish and damn the consequences? What if the consequence is the toppling of a leader who might risk leading his people to a peace settlement? What if it raises up yet another reactionary bigot who is happy to lead his faction to nowhere but the confirmation of their own worst fears and prejudices?

Those are the most pressing questions relating to "fairness" while reporting on Northern Ireland. And this is the important one: Is getting one's byline on a front page one Sunday worth bodies on the streets? It is a gray area that evades easy answers.

John O'Farrell is managing editor of Fortnight *magazine in Belfast.*

21

After Communism, Journalism

Adam Michnik

One hundred years ago Emile Zola, an outstanding French novelist, made his mark upon the 20th century by defending Alfred Dreyfus, the French army officer of Jewish roots falsely accused of espionage. In his famous letter "*J'accuse*," he wrote to the president of the French Republic: "What a spot of mud on your name—this disgraceful Dreyfus case!…I shall tell the truth, since I made an oath that I would publicize it, if the justice authorized to deal with this case does not reveal the whole truth. It is my duty to speak, since I do not want to be one of those who are guilty of this crime. The phantom of an innocent man, suffering in dreadful tortures for the crime he did not commit, would haunt me at night."

Zola stood for a man who had suffered a wrong, for enduring truths, for the idea of a tolerant state and for the good name of his homeland—France. He made the Dreyfus Affair a benchmark for public opinion. The France of yesterday spoke in attitudes toward the case: conservative, traditionalist, monarchist, Catholic and closed to strangers. But in the struggle to pronounce Dreyfus innocent, the France of tomorrow was heard: democratic, secular, republican, tolerant. It was Emile Zola who made this latter France win.

Zola formulated the standards and moral condition of writers and intellectuals for the whole century. This is why any writer, critic or journalist must see Zola's face if he is to understand his profession as something more than just a way of earning money. Thanks to Zola, for the next century, an intellectual journalist felt morally obliged to be involved in politics as a concern for the common good and not as a struggle for power.

And it remained this way for good and for bad. Zola's success became a source of courage for writers, but it also became a source of conceit. It fixed the image of an intellectual being the defender of human rights, but also the image of an intellectual being the preacher, who states what is good and what is bad in public life. This is why, during the whole of this century, one can find intellectuals not only on the front lines of struggles against totalitarian systems, but also among those praising these regimes. Following Zola, intellectuals took pride in their belief that they were charged with ripping the mask from society. The conceit bred from this pride, however, led to a blind fascination with fascism or communism, which promised to eliminate all evil from this world. An intellectual's glory and defeat in the 20th century has its source in the same great gesture by Emile Zola.

After the collapse of the Communist regime, when the free press was new in Poland, I often thought of Zola because I had to think about the experience of the 20th-century journalists who have become a powerful and integral element in modern democracy. However, I also thought about the experience of those journalists who, at the same time, became components in the corruption of modern democracy.

June 1992 shall be remembered in Polish history as the "Night of the Long Dossiers," which is a Polish paraphrase and allusion to the notorious "Night of the Long Knives," when Adolf Hitler did away with his political opponents. Fortunately, in Poland events took a gentler course.

The government that lost the parliamentary majority charged that during the epoch of dictatorship the president, the speaker of the Parliament, the minister of foreign affairs, the minister of finance and many Parliament members, among others, had been Communist secret police agents. The state was on the verge of self-destruction. It was also a moment of trial for the media. And it became obvious for journalists that we are bound by civic responsibility. This is why we almost unanimously refused to publish the list of names of those alleged agents, which the minister of the interior in the falling government constructed based on dossiers kept by Communist secret police agencies.

We decided that a dossier prepared by mortal enemies, in order to annihilate a person in a moral or physical sense, cannot be a reliable source of knowledge about an activist in a democratic opposition movement. I learned from this scandal, for the first time, that it is very easy to become an instrument in somebody else's hands and that resistance to secret manipulations must be an issue of dignity in journalism. This resistance is a concern about the ecology of our profession and the cleanliness of the environment of public debate.

I thought about this again when, in November 1995, another minister of the interior, in Parliament, accused the prime minister of the crime of spying for Soviet intelligence. The prime minister was a post-Communist, a former functionary in the Communist Party during the epoch of dictatorship. The minister of the interior was an outstanding Solidarity activist, later a political prisoner and then one of the leaders of the underground structures of the democratic opposition. Whom was I to believe? The post-Communist prime minister, who stated that he had never been a spy? Or the minister of the interior whom I had known from the time of the underground struggle against dictatorship?

In this most spectacular political scandal of recent years, the media were divided in a very characteristic way. Some—almost blindly—trusted the word of the minister of the interior. Others—also blindly—trusted the word of the prime minister. And then the leaks from the governmental secret services began. The "post-Communist" media received information that pointed to the prime minister's innocence. The "post-anti-Communist" media received information that confirmed the minister of the interior's accusations. The whole scandal, which, fortunately, did not shake Polish democracy too badly, was a great trial for the media. It also became a lesson in the distrust of governmental secret services that get involved in political struggle: It turned out that the charge of espionage directed against the post-Communist prime minister was based on totally unconvincing evidence.

Since then, I have been certain that the main enemy of a free media is the domination of ideological conviction over informative reliability. Another enemy is blindness, which leaves one able to make only trite observations. And there is one more lesson to learn from this scandal: In a democratic country, the media are tempted to use exclusive information leaked from such secret services, but these leaks are just an attempt to steer the media from the outside, to manipulate public opinion.

In light of such episodes, people ask me, "Which side are you on? Which party or alliance do you support?"

We do not see a place for ourselves in divisions understood in such a way. We are for Poland being a sovereign and lawful state, a state of parliamentary democracy and a market economy, a state that is consistent in its efforts to join the structures of Euro-Atlantic civilization and faithful to its historical identity. Only such a Republic of Poland shall be able to oppose all kinds of extreme attitudes, regardless of the name we apply to them: "black" or "red" fascism, "red" or "white" bolshevism. This is why we do not identify ourselves with any political party, whereas we are willing to treat each of them as a normal component of Polish pluralism, provided it implements the goals of Polish democracy.

We want to be, as *Gazeta*, a component of Polish democracy, one of its institutions. This is how we perceive our role in Polish public life. Additionally, we want to stick to our basic principles. Here they are: the ten commandments of a decent journalist—after communism.

1. "And God spoke all these words, saying: I am the Lord your God, who brought you out of the land of Egypt, out of the house of bondage. You shall have no other gods before me."

Our God, who led us out from bondage, has two names: Freedom and Truth. To this God we must subordinate ourselves completely. This God is jealous. He demands absolute loyalty. If we bow to other gods— the state, the nation, the family, public security—at the expense of Freedom and Truth, we shall be punished with the loss of reliability. Without reliability, one cannot be a journalist.

Freedom means equal liberties for everybody—not only for me, but also for my antagonist, for everyone who thinks differently. We must defend freedom for all because this is the essence of our profession and vocation. The only limitation to our freedom is the Truth. We are allowed to publish everything we write but we are forbidden to lie. A journalist's lie is not only a sin against the principles of our profession, it is also a blasphemy against our God. A lie always leads to enslavement. Only the Truth has liberating power.

Nevertheless, this does not mean that we can feel superior, that we are the repositories of the ultimate Truth and that we are allowed, in the name of this Truth, to silence others. Simply, we are not allowed to lie. Even if it is convenient to us or to our friends.

2. "You shall not take the name of the Lord your God in vain; for the Lord will not hold him guiltless who takes his name in vain."

Freedom and Truth are valuable and celebrated words. One must use them cautiously and seriously. The abuse of sacred words makes them cheap and banal.

We see it all the time in Poland. Under the slogan "God-Honor-Homeland," political parties run in parliamentary elections, strikes are staged, and roads are blocked by farmers who demand tax allowances. To squander these great words in electoral struggles or political smear campaigns is, in fact, to sneer at them. When we listen to these great words being transformed into political platitudes, we feel, almost physically, that, in the phrase of the revered 19th-century Polish poet Adam Mickiewicz, "a word lies to the voice, and the voice lies to thoughts." We also feel that the words lose their meaning. Language ceases to be a means of human communication and becomes a method of blackmail. If servility can be called courage, conformity called common sense, fanaticism called faithfulness to principles, and moral nihilism called tolerance, then a word becomes a means of falsifying reality. This is how Newspeak is created. Using Newspeak is like paying with forged money. We are not allowed to do this.

3. "Remember the Sabbath day, to keep it holy. Six days you shall labor, and do all your work; but the seventh day is a Sabbath to the Lord your God; in it you shall not do any work.... "

Your work is a continuous mess, performed in a state of haste and hustle. You know that a newspaper must be delivered to the kiosks early in the morning, that you must edit the news, commentary, features and photos and have it all set in columns. You do all this in a rush, under strain. It is often a routine and mechanical activity. You often lose the meaning of your work.

This is why you should remember the Sabbath, the day on which you have time for thinking. Get some distance between yourself and the world. Relax and think about the most important things. Think: Since we are all sinful, maybe you should be more moderate in throwing stones at sinners? Think: Maybe there is some truth, even though partial, in the reasoning of your adversaries? Maybe they are driven by reasons, emotions or interests that you do not understand?

Get some distance from your professional perspective. You are not only a journalist; you are also your parents' child, a parent to your children, a friend to your friends, a neighbor to your neighbors. Look at the world in a different way: from below, from above, from the side. And then look at yourself, at your pigheadedness and phobias, your easy patterns and hidden grudges. Self-examination is necessary, and you will not be able to do an honest self-examination without this.

4. "Honor your father and your mother, that your days may be long in the land which the Lord your God gives you."

Respect heritage. You do not work on a virgin land or a wasteland. Others worked here before you, and you are their descendant, heir, pupil, contestant.

This does not mean you should not be critical, but it means that respect and a knowledge of things are necessary for the fair judgment of the history of your nation, your town, your environment, your family.

What was this history like anyway? It was full of nobility and cunning, compromise and revolution, heroism and banality, tragedy and hope, conspiracy and collaboration, orthodoxy and heresy. Select individual threads from this history and construct your own tradition—a chain of persons, ideas, deeds that you want to continue. But if you do not want to become a victim of self-idealization you must remember the whole of this heritage. Your adversaries—Polish, Russian, German, Ukranian or Jewish—also stick to the commandment to honor their fathers. Try to understand them.

Self-idealization leads directly to self-delusion, to stupidity and to ideological, ethnic or religious intolerance. The foundation of human community is memory and respect for one's own mothers and fathers, for their faith, love and hope, but also for other people's mothers and fathers. Otherwise, human thought falls into the trap of lies and narcissism, or into the trap of amnesia, which makes one believe that the past is but a text, a system of signs that is not worthy of moral judgment. Czeslaw Milosz wrote about a world in which nothing really exists and nothing is true, nothing is final, nothing is worthy of love or worthy of opposition. But what meaning do life or work have then?

With not quite truth
And not quite art.
And not quite law
And not quite science,
Under not quite heaven,
On the not quite earth
The not quite guiltless
And the not quite degraded.

5. "Jesus said: Love your brother as you love yourself."

Love yourself. Value your dignity; cultivate it. Cultivate your conscience. Ask yourself difficult questions and answer them honestly. See yourself as a subject and not as an object. You should understand your responsibility for your fellow man. This fellow man may be a stranger; he may come from another family, another nation; still you should treat him the same as you treat yourself.

Reject nationalism. Orwell wrote: "By 'nationalism' I mean first of all the habit of assuming that human beings can be classified like insects and that whole blocks of millions or tens of millions of people can be confidently labeled 'good' or 'bad.' But secondly—and this is much more important—I mean the habit of identifying oneself with a single nation or other unit, placing it beyond good and evil and recognizing no other duty than that of advancing its interests. Nationalism is not to be confused with patriotism.... Patriotism is of its nature defensive, both militarily and culturally. Nationalism, on the other hand, is inseparable from the desire for power. The abiding purpose of every nationalist is to secure more power and more prestige, not for himself but for the nation or other unit in which he has chosen to sink his own individuality."

Orwell was a wise man. And Father Janusz Pasierb, the late art historian, priest, writer and poet, was wise when he spoke about love for a fellow man and explained to this fellow man: "It is good that you exist." And then added: "It is good that you are different."

Because a fellow man is different. He has a different biography, nationality, religion. Quite often he is in conflict with your biography, nation and faith. But in spite of this, love him as you love yourself. Respect his right to be different, to have another culture, another memory. Even if he was your enemy. In other words, do not generalize. Differentiate the sin from the sinner. Try to see in an adversary a partner with whom you must communicate, not an enemy whom you must destroy.

6. *"You shall not kill."*

You can kill with words; this is the poisonous charm of a journalist's work. But one can also do good with words: One can disenchant totalitarian enchantment, one can teach tolerance, one can give testimony to truth and freedom. One can analyze words. This is what the classics of Polish journalism did. Michal Glowinski, Stanislaw Baranczak, Jakub Karpinski and Teresa Bogucka were the pioneers of thorough analyses of Newspeak, of the speech of killers of words, of the speech of hatred.

Struggle with your pen, but struggle in a decent way, without hatred. Do not hit more than is needed. Do not think that you have a prescription for being just. And, especially, do not think that you can be "God's arm" when you strike a deadly blow at your adversary. When you accuse him of the lack of patriotism, of corruption, of treason, always remember that you are killing him. And the truth will be revealed anyway—and then you shall pay for your rascality. Even if it shall be only before your conscience. Do not kill. Do not do to others what you do not like others to do to you.

7. "You shall not commit adultery."

Be faithful, at least to the few principles that you consider valuable and to at least a few people to whom you owe loyalty. Do not be a hireling. Do not degrade your profession for power, for money, for "I couldn't care less." Only freedom allows you to be faithful. Moreover, the ability to be faithful—to principles, values, people—is proof of the ability to be free. Treason and hatred are the symptoms of internal emptiness that precede capitulation and enslavement. Nothing is more disgraceful than treason.

8. "You shall not steal."

Nothing is more compromising for a journalist than plagiarism. It is not only a blow to another man—it strikes the collective sense of justice and rightness.

Plagiarism permits corruption in public life; it is an act of unfairness applied as a method. Plagiarism destroys the ethos of journalism.

Manipulating truth, stupefying people—these are specific symptoms of theft, of corruption of the journalist's profession. We read great words: God, Honor, Homeland. If they are uttered by a corrupt journalist, he steals these words and deprives them of their initial meaning. Values that are turned into emblems die.

This is why journalists should tell themselves—do not steal. In other words, do not copy more than is absolutely needed.

9. "You shall not bear false witness against your neighbor."

Conflict is normal in a democratic society and state. That is why the style of this conflict, its culture and its language, are so important. We journalists are responsible, to a great degree, for this style.

It is worthwhile to realize once again certain obvious things. The commandment to reject lies ("false witness") does not mean that you

should be a free-spoken person. Not every truth must be uttered immediately, every day, regardless of the pretext. The poet Mickiewicz wrote:

There are truths which a sage tells all men,
There are some which he whispers to his nation,
There are those which he entrusts to his friends,
And there are those which he cannot disclose to anyone.

What are these truths that cannot be disclosed? They are those that
relate to the deepest secrets of conscience, truths uttered during confession, known to God and a priest and not to the reading audience.
These are truths about human intimacy, whose disclosure is a wound
inflicted upon a fellow man.

On the other hand, revealing only a part of truth about a fellow man
can be a perfidious lie about his life, like writing a biography of St.
Paul and taking into account only the period when he was Caesar's
servant and persecuted Christians.

The ability to bear true witness to one's fellow man, especially when
this fellow man is our adversary, is a basic test of our professional and
human mentality.

A person who fears to meet others in truth and freedom uses falsehood. False witness is always a symptom of weakness and lack of faith
in one's own reasoning. Just as freedom results from truth, violence
results from falsehood. A false witness has its murderous logic: It leads
from democratic debate to a cold civil war; it turns a partner into an
adversary and an adversary into a deadly enemy. The language of false
witness is a way of dehumanizing an adversary. If you are against pe-
nalizing abortion, you become similar to the authors of homicide from
Auschwitz and the Gulag. If you are for the separation of church and
state, you become an enemy of God, goodness and the truth of the
Gospel. If you refuse to discriminate against people who have different
biographies, you become a traitor to your nation.

False witness may harm or even kill a victim, but the one who utters
it is, at least, injured. False witness is a sin against a fellow man and a
blasphemy against God. It is also a capital sin against the standards of
our profession.

*10. "You shall not covet your neighbor's house; you shall not covet
your neighbor's wife."*

You shall not covet anything—including respect and popularity. If your ambition is to be popular and respected, achieve it yourself with your own work, talent and courage—and not by destroying the other person. Ambition is a wonderful and enriching feature, whereas envy is self-destructive. Envy stupefies and degrades; it kills nobility and the ability to experience higher feelings.

Envy of other persons' property leads to cowardice, to flattering the powerful and condemning the weak, to flattering crowds and participating in campaigns against the lonely. Envy infringes on the code of normal professional decency, on normal loyalty toward other people.

11. Do not mix.

I heard this additional, 11th commandment from people who like to drink alcohol (even in moderate doses). They said: Do not mix drinks. Do not mix wine with vodka, cognac with beer, plum brandy with champagne. Such mixing results in an awful hangover.

I have tried not to mix genres. Journalism is neither politics nor religious service; it is not trading in flowers nor giving a university lecture; it is not a compilation of a telephone directory nor a football match—even though it is a bit of each of these things. Each area of life has its own peculiarities, its own rules, its own ethical codes. A politician should not pretend to be a priest, a journalist should not pretend to be a politician. A businessman must seek a decent profit, and a journalist must stick to truth and freedom.

Corruption can infect all areas of public life. We know politicians who get rich where they should not get rich; we know priests who incite hatred; we know businessmen who steal and give bribes. We also know corrupt journalists who use propaganda instead of information, pseudoadvertisements instead of reliable descriptions, noisy smear campaigns instead of sensible discussions.

Am I, therefore, naive in presenting this wishful thinking addressed to myself and to my colleagues from the brotherhood of journalists? Probably I am. But when I lose this naivete, I will change my profession. As of yet, though, I do not know which profession I will choose.

Adam Michnik is editor-in-chief of Gazeta Wyborcza *in Warsaw, Poland. His essay was translated from the Polish by Elzbieta Petrajtis-O'Neill.*

22

Murray Kempton—
A Perspective for the Ages

Les Payne

When introducing Murray Kempton for induction into the American Academy of Arts and Letters, Joan Didion saluted him as a "stylist" who "in an age of conflicting correctnesses remains steadfastly, defiantly, deliberately and gloriously incorrect." She rang truest, however, when she praised Kempton as a moralist who is also a "great street reporter."

The anointing of a "street reporter," even a moral one, seemed to rustle some of the literati of the academy, who knew that Kempton actually hung out in venues frequented by politicians, prosecutors, plain folk and Mafiosi. In making his rounds on his five-speed Ross bicycle, Kempton pedaled as resolutely to the mean streets as to Park Avenue. He was as keen and courageous in dealing with muggers, including a duo that once targeted him, as he was in facing down a mayor who abused his city. As for his incorrectness, pop calipers of style could not take a true measure of Kempton's perspective, which was not so much aged as ageless.

In a *Newsday* column about Kempton's Academy induction, which I attended as his guest, I compared him with one of his heroes, H.L. Mencken. Born in Baltimore, both writers loved politics and, though men of *belles lettres*, were at bottom newspapermen. (Mencken, of course, refused to accept a 1935 invitation to join the Academy, the veritable Matterhorn of the fine arts in America then called the National Institute of Arts and Letters.) Paying Kempton what I knew to be a supreme compliment, I wrote that he was "cut from the same cloth as the Sage of Baltimore, though by a finer tailor."

This last point drew a mild Kempton rebuke in an otherwise gentle, handwritten note. Such was the nature of our relationship. "Some fool observed to me yesterday that you had suggested that my work is more finely tailored than Mencken's. I know better and said so. You only meant that my clothes are more self-conscious than Mencken's, which may be for the better or the worse; you and I know too well that my prose is more self-conscious than Mencken's, which is rather far for the worse."

Their prose styles aside, I had meant to suggest that Kempton had a richer intellect and sharper judgment. Though he lacked Mencken's diamond-hard clarity, he wrote with a greater measure of that other quality so critical to the newspaperman: fairness.

The two great peaks of columnizing in this republic, for this or any other century, are Mencken and Kempton. Yet the issue of fairness, that quality by which the journalist weighs his facts and subjects with an eye looking beyond balance toward justness, is a key feature separating these two giants of American journalism.

Mencken staked no claim to fairness. In fact, he wrote as if he saw some great virtue in being unfair. Once he spit on his hands and had at a subject with hammer and tongs, the Baltimore Sage gave no quarter. Such was the beat of the blood of this *enfant terrible* that, whether profiling a politician or reviewing a book, he had, for example, banned from his vocabulary for life the word "outstanding."

Yet fairness up to the limits of the endurable was the very bedrock of Murray Kempton's journalism. The great grandson of an Episcopal bishop, he worked from a firm moral center, carefully weighing such facts and characters as he encountered against a personal standard of ethics more immutable than that of the courts and certainly of journalism. Unlike those journalists who merely preached about afflicting the comfortable, Kempton practiced it—along with his penchant for comforting the afflicted. Inspiring what William Safire called a "graceful iconoclasm," Kempton spent a career lancing powerful men not with Mencken's broadax but with a rapier. And he was careful never to pierce them when they were down. He sliced Roy Cohn. He slivered Richard Nixon until he fell from grace, at which point they somehow became friends. When Gov. Mario Cuomo once asked how he might get Kempton "to love me," Sydney Schanberg advised him, "Governor, why don't you try getting yourself indicted?"

It would have been impossible for Kempton to write with the reckless savagery Mencken employed even upon the death of a worn-out enemy. "Has it been duly marked by historians that William Jennings Bryan's last secular act on this globe of sin was to catch flies?" Mencken wrote the day the populist leader died shortly after the Scopes "Monkey Trial" where he had defended the Bible against Darwin's theory of evolution. "A curious detail, and not without its sardonic overtones. He was the most sedulous fly catcher in American history, and in many ways the most successful. His quarry, of course, was not *Musca domestica* but *Homo neandertalensis*." He called Bryan a "charlatan, a mountebank, a zany without sense or dignity" who fittingly died in a "one-horse Tennessee village, beating off flies and gnats...Bryan lived too long and descended too deeply into the mud."

As Mencken reigned from his mountain kingdom as Avenging Angel, Kempton plied his craft on the streets as Recording Angel.

While it bothered Kempton somewhat that he was unable to write such a piece as Mencken's postmortem attack on William Jennings Bryan, he still admired the dangerous infidel and considered "In Memoriam" one of Mencken's best pieces. "He showed great courage," Kempton said about the Bryan piece first written as an obit in *The Evening Sun* of Baltimore. "I would never have that much guts. It bothers me. You should always write as if you're going to get hit by a truck." Fairness and his respect for journalistic etiquette stayed Kempton's hand even in the attack while Mencken was totally unafraid to violate all proprieties. "It's hard for me to write about Reagan as he should be written about." This was in 1985. This is not to say, however, that Kempton's cultivated sense of fairness was not tough-minded, muscular and shot through and through with grit. A decade later, in *The New York Review of Books*, he blasted the political system as "one party with two wings, the old Republicans, who are insensitive and stony, and the new Democrats, who are insensitive and flaccid."

No politician who felt Kempton's lash, including Reagan and certainly George Wallace, Mayor Koch and George Bush, was moved to beg for more. Fraternization was out of the question. It was Kempton who taught political reporters a fundamental lesson most have never learned, to wit, that "it is impossible to judge any public figure with the proper detachment once you begin calling him by his first name."

It was, finally, Bill Clinton who would provide for Kempton a critical test of nerves if not his sense of fairness. Early on, Clinton the "draft evader" convinced the war veteran in Kempton that he was morally unfit to be president. In the early going, with Gov. Clinton steamrolling into Madison Square Garden to be anointed as his party's

1992 candidate, Kempton skipped a Democratic convention for the first time since World War II. However, as it turned out, he had presciently reserved himself a ringside seat in Dallas at the concurrent launching of Ross Perot's campaign, which eventually pinched the 19 percent of the election vote that sent President Bush packing. "Whose decision was it to send Murray to Dallas?" asked an impressed Sydney Schanberg stranded in New York City. I owned up to the decision but confessed that it was Murray's idea.

Throughout the Clinton first term, Kempton, from his parapet in New York, savaged the president up and down Pennsylvania Avenue. Uneasy with his requisite lancing of this severely flawed commander in chief lacking any trace of principles and honor, he preferred to write about him at a great distance.

Again, in 1996, Kempton conspired to skip the 1996 Democratic renomination in Chicago by absconding to Georgia. Begging off assignments to profile the president, he worried on election eve that by electing a president he personally loathed "a high quotient of voters may hate themselves in the morning." In a show of his essential sense of fairness, however, Kempton added, "They oughtn't to. They had no realistic alternative. A preference for Dole and the picturesque belongs to those tastes that have become peculiar for being out of date."

Kempton's 18th-century sense of honor demanded that a man regret a discreditable deed, even if it had worked and he had gotten away with it. In writing about the book of Dick Morris, "the president's Machiavelomaniacal political strategist" who engineered Clinton's re-election, Kempton zeroed in on one telling aspect that separates these two high-flying philanderers:

"All through the same year that Morris was imbuing Clinton with the incenses of morality, he was employing a young woman of purchasable virtue to let him suck her toes and such other anatomical portions as the devil might suggest. When he was caught at it and Clinton sent Erskine Bowles to tell him to go hence, Morris remembers sobbing, 'What the hell did I do that he wasn't accused of doing four years ago?'

'You've admitted it's true,' Bowles replied."

While being "too smart to admit anything" made President Clinton a winner with the voters for the moment, Kempton condemned him as a sinner with "God frequently on [his] lips and a habitual tolerance for the seven deadly sins contending for attention within."

"LBJ was haunted by his sins," Kempton said shortly after falling fatally ill. "Clinton has absolutely no sense of guilt."

Decades ago Kempton as columnist daily set to measuring government behavior against his lofty standards. In the 1950s he almost alone stood up to respectable society and defended Communists who were being trampled, in a thousand ways, by a timorous populace lathered up by a clique of paranoid government agents. It troubled him that his colleagues in the craft refused at first to stand with him and fight. "I think they were wrong, and that they neglected their education. All through that period, liberals were saying, 'I'm an anti-Communist, but [Sen. Joseph] McCarthy has gone too far.' I think it was a failure of character. It's very American."

Under a key principle of fairness that Kempton adapted for his work during that period, he vigorously defended not only the wrong man arrested but also the right man arrested and abused. Time and time again, he argued that even if the FBI had properly identified people as Communists, it did not justify their being jailed, thrown "out of jobs and housing projects, off pensions, into tax courts." This campaign was waged against "fellow-travelers," many of whom Kempton felt were misidentified, near indigent and woefully deprived of means to earn a living. "Is there," Kempton demanded to know, "any better measure of a nation than the way it treats the helpless?"

This fight for the underdog Kempton took from his defense of Communists during the first half of the 1950s to his witness against Southern Justice in the second half of the decade. Often alone, inciting the sheriff's men, he covered the Mississippi trial of the white men who lynched Emmett Till and helped immortalize the victim's uncle, Mose Wright, who had to flee north immediately for his life after pointing out the killers in court. A strong and early chronicler of the civil rights movement, Kempton covered Autherine Lucy's brief desegregation of the University of Alabama and the bold emergence of the Rev. Martin Luther King Jr., which ushered in the bloody transformation of the Old South.

"There are few things to say about those years," Kempton once wrote, "except that the Southern Negro began them as victim and ended them as healer."

Kempton's prose was crystal clear in those days. Toward the end, however, he occasionally came up on charges of lapsing into a scholarly obtuseness barely accessible to the average newspaper reader. "Have you ever tried to read Murray Kempton's report from Atlanta?" a

Newsday reader inquired when the columnist was daily covering the trial of Wayne Williams, who was later convicted in the Atlanta "child murders" case.

Upon reaching Kempton, this critique offered him a chance to explain, defensively, his attempts to cover fairly those trials where strategy is as much in question as guilt.

"When you're covering a trial," he wrote his editor in response, "you're dealing with a defendant and he has a right to be safeguarded against rushes to judgment no matter how small the chance that yours will do him the slightest damage. And when you don't know the facts and have to wait until the jury hears such of them as prosecutor and defense counsel serve up...[t]he only thing to do is to try and get the atmosphere of the court, guess at strategies and otherwise just do your best to get ready for learning the case. At the same time you have to write; that's what the office sent you there for. So you write and, of course, you're murky, especially if you're like myself and murky enough when you know the story."

Most trials, however, especially those on his home turf, presented no such mystery for Kempton. A master of the courtroom, he seemed to work well ahead of both prosecution and defense.

Whether covering trials or political conventions or commenting on local and world affairs, Kempton—who died at the age of 79 in the spring of 1997—was the most revered voice in journalism. In a craft that eschews hero worshipping, Murray Kempton spent his latter decades as an unwilling guru for otherwise heathen journalists.

Hinting at his essential decency—and fairness—Jules Feiffer, who was inducted into the Academy with Kempton, memorialized him the week of his death. In one of the artist's comic panels, he has Richard Nixon say of Kempton, "If he had lived a little longer, he might have even written something nice about Clinton."

Les Payne is assistant managing editor, national, foreign and science, for Long Island's Newsday. *He is writing a biography of Malcolm X.*

23

Seeking Higher Ground with Tony Lukas

Joan Diver and Colin Diver

Tony Lukas came into our lives in October 1976, unexpected and unbidden. Colin took the phone call in the dining room of our shabby Victorian. "My name is Tony Lukas," said the unfamiliar voice. "I'm writing a book about busing in Boston." The stranger explained that he was a writer and former reporter, that he was looking for three families to profile in his new book, and that mutual friends had recommended that he call us. Colin recoiled at the unwanted intrusion:

"We don't live in Boston anymore," he said. "We just moved to the suburbs. We have nothing more to do with busing. That's all behind us."

"I know," Tony answered. "That's why I need to talk to you." Frustration almost poured through the receiver. "I must have interviewed 40 families, but I can't find the right one. I've been told you have a story to tell. Just let me talk to you. Once."

Something in the resonance of that baritone voice, the sincerity of its pleading, broke through Colin's resistance. "Okay, just once."

Eight years later we got our first look at Tony's 1,300-page manuscript entitled *Common Ground: A Turbulent Decade in the Lives of Three American Families*. The first chapter was titled, simply, "Diver." There we were, after literally hundreds of hours of interviews and discussions, reduced to a chapter heading. As we turned the pages, we experienced the shock of seeing our names as subjects of sentences, objects of others' purposes, authors of actions and quotations. Yet, as we read, the characters bearing our names assumed a remarkably familiar shape and feel. Tony Lukas had recreated us in the medium of the written word. And, even more remarkably, we realized that in the process he had helped to make us whole.

Speaking at his memorial service last June, we reminisced publicly about the very intimate experience of working with Tony. We praised him for his doggedness as an investigator, his balance as a portraitist, his sympathy as a listener, his faithfulness as a friend. At the reception afterward, writers and reporters came up to us shaking their heads. They expressed amazement that a journalist's subjects would even harbor such feelings, much less share them with a roomful of strangers. "The subjects of my work probably hate me," one said. "They certainly would never eulogize me."

What was it, we asked ourselves in the weeks that followed, that prompted such remarks? How did Tony Lukas get perfect strangers to open themselves up to him? How did he manage to win their trust and even affection while laying bare their private lives?

On the surface, Tony Lukas possessed in abundance the classic reportorial skills. He was obsessed with accuracy. He would go to the ends of the earth, it sometimes seemed, to track down a missing detail or verify an uncertain point. Tony asked Colin about our first encounter with Boston's South End, the multiracial neighborhood that would soon become our home. Colin recalled stopping at the South End home of a co-worker to pick up gloves and bats on the way to a softball game. Tony suddenly stopped Colin in mid-sentence: "What was the name of the softball team? Who played what positions? Did you wear a uniform? Who won the game?"

"Stop!" Colin finally protested in frustration. "I can't remember. That was eight years ago!"

Two weeks later, Tony returned triumphantly with answers to every one of his questions, pieced together from half a dozen interviews.

On another occasion, as Colin was recounting the story of chasing a mugger with a baseball bat, Tony became fascinated with the bat. After learning that Colin had saved it from his Little League days, Tony scoured the archives of a suburban newspaper until he found the box scores of the games.

Tony spent weeks doing genealogical research on his three families: the Twymons, the Debnams and the Divers. In the course of tracing Joan's father's roots back to 18th-century Scotland, he solved a long-standing mystery about the spelling of the family surname. (One ancestor, upon moving to Boston, had changed *McKechnie* to *Makechnie* so he wouldn't be mistaken for an immigrant Irishman.)

But Tony wanted much more than accuracy. He wanted authenticity. "How did you feel?" he would often ask. "What was it like?" He wanted to recapture not just the words and the actions of the moment, but its psychological essence, its dramatic feel. Colin told Tony about his anger upon learning that his boss, Kevin White, planned to run for governor of Massachusetts only two years after being elected mayor of Boston. With assistance from Tony's gentle but persistent cross-examination, Colin recalled the time and place when the mayor first told him. But that was not enough for Tony. "Try to recall what you were doing," he said.

Colin ransacked his memory: "Something about popcorn. Yes, we were making popcorn, in the mayor's kitchen. The mayor was just nonchalantly shoveling popcorn in his face while he was telling me he was abandoning the city." And so it would go until Tony had what the scene required—the ironic juxtaposition of popcorn and betrayal.

Understandably, the dramatist in Tony made him want to find evidence of intersections in his characters' stories. Sometimes he looked too hard. "Isn't it possible," he would say, "that you attended the big civil rights demonstration at Harvard while Colin was in law school? Isn't it possible that one of the Twymon kids was in the group that hassled you on the street corner near your house that night? Isn't it possible that you were at the bicentennial concert on the Esplanade the night that the Debnams were defending their house against a gang of racist thugs?"

But the journalist in him would always pull him back from the edge of manufactured history. Yes, we might say, it is possible, but not likely. Tony would shrug his shoulders and shift his gaze inward, as if thinking: There is a pattern in history. I just have to find it. Deep within him, he knew that storytellers' inventions rarely match the irony or the drama of history's own logic.

A devotion to accuracy and authenticity may be necessary conditions for great journalism. But they are not sufficient. The question remains: How does a journalist get his subjects to open up? What was it about Tony Lukas that prompted people to peel away layer after layer of memory while his tape recorder hummed quietly? Part of the answer is, of course, his professionalism, his care and precision. His books and articles all bespoke a reverence for the truth. But often the truth is the last thing a subject wants to reveal. When Tony arrived in our lives that October night in 1976, we were fleeing from the truth. The last thing we wanted was to tell a perfect stranger about our neighbor who kept a gun by his bedside; about the neighborhood feud that erupted when Joan urged the police to prosecute prostitutes; about our describing the

South End as "unlivable" in a letter to the mayor; about the bitter re-criminations of our son when we told him we were moving. But all this poured out of us and into Tony's tape recorder—and from his tape recorder onto the pages of a best-selling book and the screenplay for a CBS docudrama. Why?

We suspect that it was Tony's own struggle that gave us permission to share ours; his own vulnerability reassured ours. As an interviewer, Tony sometimes fumbled for the right word or phrase. His questions were often halting, tentative, almost apologetic. His questions evolved organically in response to the answers, never formulaic or programmed. One sensed that we were engaged in a mutual quest—we, to find answers to his relentless questions; he, to find meaning for his own life in the tribulations of others. He seemed most animated when we talked about the personal moral dilemmas of our urban existence. Why, given our family histories and beliefs, had we not been more active in the civil rights movement? How did we, as believers in desegregation, feel about pulling strings to get our son reassigned from a school in a mostly black neighborhood to our own already integrated school? How did we feel about gentrifying longtime low-income residents right out of the neighborhood?

Those were painful questions. Yet, Tony always asked them so gently. He always listened so intently, without a trace of judgment, as we struggled to answer them.

Tony's style of journalism naturally opened him up to two criticisms. Some felt that he got personally too close to his subjects to remain objective. Others faulted him for failing to inform his narrative with his own thesis or analysis. We think both criticisms are off the mark.

Tony did indeed get close to his subjects. We, like the Twymons and the McGoffs, the two other families depicted in *Common Ground*, spoke of him as our friend. We spent many hours with him, at our home and his, at restaurants and clubs, when there was no tape recorder or steno pad in evidence.

Yet, *Common Ground* was always our common bond. The unremitting quest to find meaning in the ordinariness of our daily lives was always the subject or the subtext of our encounters. The very fact that Tony seemed to us to be sharing in that quest gave us permission to open up to him in a way that we never would with a more disinterested observer. Helping us to discover the truth that we had hidden from ourselves helped us to reveal it to the world.

And, yes, Tony's writing was not highly conceptual or analytical in the usual sense. *Common Ground* is 651 pages of densely described personal and public histories, painstakingly researched and beautifully written. But "what is the bottom line?" people would always ask. "Was busing a success or a failure? Was the culprit racism or classism?" In interviews after the book was released, Tony would stumble to give an answer that would satisfy his interrogator. It was a futile effort. People want simple heuristics for understanding complex phenomena; they want crisp guidelines for sorting out difficult moral conundrums. Tony gave them complexity, ambiguity, struggle.

But he did not give them randomness. He did not give them self-indulgent detail. His research and his writing were powerfully guided by an inchoate belief that complex social movements are rooted in the most primordial of human conflicts. What drew Tony to the topic of busing in Boston was not some intellectual abstraction about educational policy or constitutional law or social fragmentation. He cared about all those things, and we talked endlessly about them. But to Tony the busing controversy was, at its core, a family feud. He often remarked how busing pitted blue-collar Irish Catholics against their "lace-curtain" upper-crust cousins. But he also saw it as pitting black against black, "Yankee" against Yankee, brother against sister, mother against son. And, at the most basic level, he must have seen it as the working out of an inner conflict that each of us tries to contain within our own heart—the same conflict that he tried, in the end unsuccessfully, to contain within his own heart.

The final chapter of *Common Ground* tells the story of our decision to move out of Boston—a metaphor for a generation's moral exhaustion. With his unerring eye for symbolism, Tony ended the book by describing how Colin began his suburban exile one winter, in his basement workshop, cutting hundreds of pieces to repair the antique colonial fence that surrounded our property:

"When spring came, [Colin] spent evenings and weekends fitting the pieces together, then laying on three coats of white paint. In early June the job was done, the intricate junction of peg and hole sealing off the Divers' perimeter, rearing its ivory spine against the world."

We wept when we first read those words fourteen years ago. When we read them again after learning of Tony's suicide, we thought of how he had devoted his journalist's life to "fitting the pieces together,...the intricate junction of peg and hole"—the painstaking and painful process of his uncompromising search for meaning. In the end, the meaning that he helped others to find eluded him.

Joan Diver, a spiritual healer currently working on a spiritual autobiography, and Colin Diver, dean and Bernard G. Segal Professor of Law at the University of Pennsylvania Law School, were profiled in J. Anthony Lukas' Common Ground.

24

Speaking of Editors

Interviews with Jerry Ceppos, Shelby Coffey III, Max Frankel,
James Hoge, Dave Lawrence and Geneva Overholser

Interviews by Jennifer Kelley

MSJ: *Describe your overall experience of coverage—has it been fair or unfair?*

Jerry Ceppos: My experience confirms what every editor knows in his or her gut, that there are good reporters and not so good reporters out there. It's just what you would tell your colleagues over dinner and probably wouldn't tell other people.

MSJ: *What characteristics would you attribute to unfair reporting? Would you say bad reporting stems from laziness or maliciousness or what?*

Ceppos: I do not attribute unfair reporting to malice. And that's probably the main difference between what I would say and what newsmakers who aren't journalists would say. You often hear that there's a hidden agenda and all that, and I do not believe that to this day.

MSJ: *Can you describe an experience that you would characterize as especially fair? What qualities made the reporter's actions stand out in your mind?*

Ceppos: The best reporters are a bit insecure. One of my very best experiences was with a reporter, Todd Purdum of *The New York Times*, who came in saying, "Gee, I haven't really followed this story (*San Jose Mercury News*' coverage of the CIA/drug connection) at all. I really need to catch up." He peppered me with questions not just about that day's developments but about background. Then he rented a motel room nearby and called me at least two or three times with more questions. I do not think he was doing that to pretend innocence. I think he was doing it because he was worried. His story was a model of fairness and accuracy, and was also deep. It would have been easy for him to ignore background and some of the underbrush of the story that he was writing, but he didn't. His story had depth and it was fair and accurate, and I attribute that to his—my word, not his—insecurity. He was very careful.

Good reporters take extra steps. Good reporters are a little bit nervous about what they write.

I'm beginning to conclude that sometimes it might be better not to be super immersed in a story. What I mean by that is that some of the people who cover the intelligence community did some of the reporting that wasn't the best in our situation. And someone like Todd Purdum came at it totally cold, scared that he was cold and not only had no preconceptions, but asked the very most basic questions. And this runs counter to everything we think we know.

It's better to have a reporter deeply grounded in a subject. But there is something to be said for coming to a story with no preconceptions whatsoever, if you're then smart enough to ask the right questions.

MSJ: *On the other side, can you describe an instance of unfair coverage and the factors that came into play there?*

Ceppos: I'm listening more carefully now when people say the following to me: "When you call me for quick quotes after the story is framed or even written, it doesn't serve much of a purpose."

I encountered at least two cases where I was stunned to see that I had been called on the eve of publication of stories that were thousands of words long. Had I realized that I was an insert, and I literally was in one case, I would have said "Your story's already done, you don't need anything from me." I'm so hesitant to say that because it's the kind of sour-grapes quote you get from press haters, but I believe some of them have a valid point. If you're not going to talk to key characters before the story is 99 percent written, then you've got a fairness problem.

I would say that the unsophisticated news source is really on dangerous ground. I mean, I know how the system works, and I had trouble navigating it. I would hate to be the accidental newsmaker. If a plane crashes into their house, I would tell people they probably should not grant interviews—and I hate to say that—if they're not sophisticated.

The final thing that constitutes unfairness is so elementary it's shocking. And that is, there's got to be a procedure for fair handling of complaints. I believe that our newspaper or our staff adheres to our rules— I hope—which stipulate that if somebody calls to complain about a story you've done, you're supposed to pass it on to an editor, rather than be put in the position of arguing with the complainer.

We have an occasional column called "Another Point of View" for when somebody thinks we're just totally off base and it's not just a factual correction, it's the whole framing thing. I think most people would tell you we bend over backwards to give display to longer letter-to-the-editor pieces.

MSJ: *In light of these experiences, what do you tell your staff and what would you convey to your colleagues in the news media?*

Ceppos: We've been having a series of fairness and accuracy conversations with the staff. We've had eight of them in the last two months, and we're trying to publish something. One of the things that came out of our seminars is that we need to listen to people who are telling us things. Listen well when people say you may be off base. Be insecure and worry about what you're writing. Consider drastic steps like reading the story, or parts of the story, back to the source.

At our paper, one of the chief proponents of reading a story to the sources is an investigative reporter and a Pulitzer Prize-winner, Pete Carey. Pete did a story about E. coli bacteria and read it back to the juice company, Odwalla Inc. And Pete has the confidence to say, "You know, this story has a lot of science in it. I didn't study biology or whatever science it might be. Let me read it to you, and I have the right to tell you you're full of it if I don't want to make the changes you suggest, Mr. Source, but I am confident enough to read it back to you."

Be willing to take some unusual steps and think about fairness and accuracy in different ways. And clearly, and this is the easiest one, correct almost everything anyone points out to you, in a factual way. I go around the newsroom saying, "We haven't run enough corrections today." In a newspaper as large as ours, there must be more than two or three things that we got wrong. So as a result we also have a very long corrections column, and I think that's great. I think we should prime the pump and encourage *more* corrections. And I don't think there should be an onus, unless it's a grievous error, on the reporter. I think we ought to admit, just the way doctors should but sometimes don't, that we're in a profession that's going to make some mistakes, so let's correct them. It's easier to correct our mistakes than it is to correct a doctor's mistakes—usually.

* * *

MSJ: *How would you characterize your overall experience of coverage—has it been fair or unfair?*

Shelby Coffey III: I'm reminded of a quote attributed to Edward R. Murrow, that when newspeople are written about, it's not that they're thin-skinned, it's that they have no skin at all. Naturally, as an editor, you've probably got some quibbles and other ideas, and occasionally there'll be a piece that probably you could take more than small exception to, but that's in the nature of the media world.

MSJ: *Do you recall any pieces that were remarkable in their fairness? By that we don't necessarily mean flattering or positive, of course, but fair in the way that they were reported?*

Coffey: The pieces I remember were ones where you'd be pleasantly surprised that a reporter had really spent some time and caught some of the subtleties and the different forces at work in a situation or in your organization. If you're on the inside of a story, you often see many more elements and ramifications than are going to be able to be grasped generally by a reporter who has a limited amount of time and a deadline. There have been many times when I felt there was good, fair coverage because I could see the reporter working hard to get those elements.

MSJ: *How about pieces where you thought the reporting was unfair—what made them that way to your thinking?*

Coffey: At one point early on after I was named editor at the *Los Angeles Times*, there was a set of profiles of me that were all done in a relatively brief period of time at four different publications by different people. It was at a time when the basic facts of my life were all pretty much the same. And what was interesting to me as someone who had written and edited profiles was the way in which you would see which elements of the story appealed to the authors. Certain people's (and to some extent their publication's) personalities come into play in what they would say was important. And so you would see some interesting differences in the results.

The question of fairness depends to some extent on the personality of the reporter and sometimes on the publication. There are some places that want highly opinionated, colorful slams at larger and established publications, and you just have to deal with that. That is what a little publication in a town will do with big publications. I saw that in Washington; I saw that in Dallas and in Los Angeles. You have to understand that and not be unduly concerned about it.

That is reflective of something you see now more often in various kinds of discourse—from political discourse to certain kinds of television talk shows: a coarsening of argument, a sort of scorched-earth type of opinion-mongering in which whoever is your opponent or whatever is your target never did anything right. It's entertaining at times but often leaves out the complexities of truth that are what we should strive for in journalism. I don't think getting at the truth is a vanished virtue, but there are certainly problems.

MSJ: *In light of these experiences, what additional recommendations would you make to your colleagues in the news media in the interest of fairness?*

Coffey: As the journalist working on the story, in instances where there would be at least some elements of controversy or criticism, you should put yourself in the place of the person or the institution being written about. If you could say that the reporter had in fact developed a clear and smart working knowledge of the issues—if the person being written about could say, "At least he gave me my say. He allowed the chance to put my perspective on it," and if the subject could finish the article feeling that the tone and nuances had a sense of balance, then you were accomplishing fairness.

Working with words, we are often going to be dealing with things that are approximations. So there is a real matter of it being incumbent on us to go the extra mile.

A friend of mine who is a prominent TV journalist was talking about how he had talked to one world leader who had said that he thought it would be good whenever someone was brought to the head of politics in an important country that they be taken out and shown a nuclear bomb test, so they would understand the nature of being macho and making warlike sounds.

My friend, who has really had a lot of press written about him over the years, said he wished that every journalism student or cub reporter would have a deep personal profile written about her, in which the reporter's beginning stance was one of suspicion and ferreting about for all sorts of hypocrisies. He felt that that would be, in the same way that the world leader suggested, a useful exercise.

* * *

MSJ: *Describe your overall experience of coverage—has it been fair or unfair?*

Max Frankel: We've all encountered unfairness, which is when somebody writes something about you to which you would have had a clear and easy response had you only been called—and that's happened to me even from some highly responsible papers once in a while. It just reminds you of the importance of the rule that we try to live by, which is to always give people a chance to comment, particularly when there's something negative being said about them. In general, if you're going to mention somebody's name in print, and he or she has been talked about by someone else, the decent thing and proper thing to do is to call them and let them put their mind to the same issue.

MSJ: *Can you describe an instance of unfair coverage and the factors that came into play?*

Frankel: Once I was called on something, which we tried to clarify, and the writer just wouldn't be educated. That was really shocking, and it was a significant writer at a significant publication, and we really cared a lot about it.

It was a perfectly good article, nice and straightforward, that suddenly asserted that I was resigning as editor one year earlier than people had expected because my wife had had breast cancer and I was worried about her. In fact I was pointing out that my offer to resign and the scheduling of my resignation at age 64 had occurred on my 63rd birthday, a year earlier, which was before she was ever diagnosed with breast cancer, and so illness really had nothing to do with it. Obviously somebody in the office or elsewhere was speculating that it did, and the author preferred his version and went into print with it. I resented it deeply, because it also hurt my wife, who didn't want to feel responsible somehow for my resignation. The writer may have intended it as complimentary—here I was putting my personal life ahead of my ambitions. I don't think it was meant as an insult, it was just hurtful because we had been given a chance to explain it away, and neither of us was believed. That was upsetting.

But by and large I've been dealt with fairly. You always have trouble recognizing yourself in the way others see you, but that's been true since childhood, since I learned that I wouldn't even recognize my own voice when I heard it. All that that tells you is that when people finally call to complain that they have not been dealt with fairly, give them a fair hearing. It may happen that you have done unto them what has been done unto you. Beyond that, all journalism is a simple, quick cut at reality and is bound to cause people who figure in the news to feel that they have not been wholly or fully represented. That's almost inevitable.

MSJ: *Can you think of an experience that stands out for being particularly fair?*

Frankel: I remember once I put my foot in it. I got angry at a feminist group that was attacking *The New York Times* because we didn't have enough stories or pictures of women on page 1. And I blew my stack at Betty Friedan and some other people who were involved. And then someone—I think it was Eleanor Randolph, then at *The Washington Post*—called me to get me to comment further. And I put my foot in it by saying, trying to make a serious point, that if women were managing the world they'd be more often on page 1 of the *Times*, and it's unfair to compare us to the publication that deals with entertainment issues where women figure more prominently than in the politics that we cover. And I went on to say something to the effect that if we were covering more tea parties, women would figure more prominently in our news.

All hell broke loose—did I think that women are only fit for tea parties? The image I really had in mind was from when I was a foreign correspondent and all the wives of the diplomats always complained that they were unpaid adjuncts to diplomacy because they had to give all these tea parties. Eleanor jumped on this thing and made a big issue of it and all hell broke loose in my own newsroom. Women came around wearing tea bags as earrings, and we had a jolly old time trying to explain myself for a flip comment. When I got home that night and I told my wife about it, she said, "Oh, you're going to get in trouble!" And I did. I was fairly called to task for a sloppy comment, an anachronistic comment, and was fairly dealt with, even though I got into deep trouble.

Little things like that are revealing. It taught me that my mind lived in an era and in a generation such that the new generation didn't know what I was talking about. That in itself was a useful education.

MSJ: *In light of these experiences, what would you convey to your colleagues in the news media about fair reporting?*

Frankel: Every story, precisely because it is a summary of something, ultimately conveys an idea or two or a theme or two. I like to think that before they sit down to write the final draft, reporters or writers ask themselves, "What is it that I am saying here and what impression am I conveying?" I think you have to start simply by asking what is the underlying theme rather than just what do the words in quotes say. Just by asking, "What is it I'm trying to say here?" reporters and writers end up reminding themselves to think of whether their writing is fair to the subject.

* * *

MSJ: *In your career as an editor, how would you describe your overall experience with being covered? Has it tended to be fair or unfair?*

James Hoge: It tends to break down into two chapters in my case. The first chapter is the many years when I was at the *Chicago Sun-Times*, first as editor and then as publisher. Generally the coverage was intended to be fair and for the most part was. When it wasn't, it was usually due to sloppiness or inadequate reporting. Some reporters rely too much on clips. Clips include impressions of one particular reporter or from one set of circumstances. They can take on an unwarranted permanence unless reporters and writers take a fresh look themselves.

The second chapter is the *New York Daily News*. The reporting on the *Daily News* and my role was on the whole an effort to be fair. I think it sometimes broke down during the very acrimonious labor negotiations and the strike. From time to time there were reports in competing newspapers that were driven by market competitiveness rather than by objectivity. I think some were slanted because of emotional support for one union or another vs. an objective look at the situation. And I say that as much about what was ignored. For example, there was a rather sustained campaign of illegalities during the strike—news of which was, to my opinion, underreported till late in the game and after repeated complaints from us.

A second observation, particularly from the *Daily News* days, is that the level of economic understanding is pretty low in a good part of the press. As to television and electronic journalism, there just simply isn't the time or the inclination to provide much economic, historical or market context. TV reports tend to be claims vs. claims, which leaves news accounts vulnerable to bald-faced assertions of one kind or another. I think if you were to try to understand what was going on at the *Daily News* through what you saw on television, you'd have a great deal of difficulty.

MSJ: *That pretty much covers your encounters with unfair coverage. Do you recall any examples of particularly fair coverage and what elements made it fair?*

Hoge: After much prodding, *The New York Times* did a rather extensive look at violence attendant to the *Daily News* strike—but late in the process, actually when it was almost all over. A lengthy piece in a Saturday edition attempted to be complete and fair-minded.

MSJ: *In sum, then, is there anything you've learned from these experiences that you would like to convey to your colleagues in the press, or things you tell your staff that might resonate?*

Hoge: Maybe it's nostalgia on my part, but I have the feeling that in the past generation there was a tougher attempt by the gatekeepers—editors at various levels—to see that high standards of fairness, accuracy and public relevance were met. Maybe it's just that we tend to think our time was better than the one that followed us. But if I've learned anything, it's that you need an ongoing commitment to fairness, completeness and accuracy that is constantly demonstrated in word and deed by the people in charge of the editorial product. Reporters are capable of doing it themselves but providing the environment in which that is a necessity, where that is the way in which you are judged, makes a big difference.

* * *

MSJ: *Describe your overall experience of coverage—has it been fair or unfair?*

Dave Lawrence: Over the course of the years—this is a sad commentary—what I've been largely satisfied with is simply not to be burned. I'm not looking for coverage or needing coverage. And reporters, when they're interviewing other newspaper people, frankly tend not to give them the benefit of the doubt. I think one of the "values" of our craft is that you've got to bend over backwards to make sure people don't think you're a wimp or a pushover or favoring your own. So the coverage I have seen of myself or this newspaper has ranged from the acceptable but not deeply insightful most of the time to what I regard as monstrously skewed by someone's prejudice.

So much of the coverage is shallow. I'm always stunned at the number of simple facts that are wrong—literally wrong.

I deal with a lot of reporters, and I'm generally very high on my craft. I like the people I work with; I think newspaper people are intelligent, caring, idealistic—all great qualities. But I also run into a lot of reporters who, by the time they call me, have already made up their mind about what the truth is. And I've been in the business long enough that I know quite quickly who has made up his or her mind and who hasn't—who will give you a fair shot to get across your story and who doesn't.

Since we're in the business of asking questions, I work hard never to refuse to answer questions. So I respond to everybody who calls me about anything.

At my own newspaper and other newspapers, I know extraordinary people whom I would trust totally with their sense of facts and fairness and context and thoughtfulness, but I think those are not the overwhelming majority in our business. I have almost never worked with someone who I thought was just plain incompetent or an ideologue, but rather I have seen so many people who were frankly not very committed to finding out what the truth of the matter is and who were awfully quick to buy a quick and early solution.

MSJ: *What factors have played into what you perceive as unfair coverage?*

Lawrence: I don't think it's sensationalism as much as I think frequently it's intellectual laziness. I also think that too often people in our business don't realize the enormous power they have to set all kinds of images. They just literally don't realize the power of the words. I spoke to a reporter this very afternoon, and she had used in a story the word *hangers-on* which, where I come from, is a pejorative term. She's a good person, and my message to her was, "You're too good a reporter to do this kind of stuff." The best kind of reporting gets the facts out there and lets readers make up their own minds about whether this person is a hanger-on or not. I said, "How'd you like to be regarded as a hanger-on at *The Miami Herald*? I don't think you'd like that." It's just sort of cliché journalism. Journalism is far more than simply getting the facts right. You could have the facts right and not be very close to the truth.

MSJ: *Can you describe a time when you were covered that stands out in your mind for its fairness?*

Lawrence: There may well be one, but I can't think of a piece when I thought, "Boy, this person really got to the heart of the matter." I have seen many pieces that were technically accurate, but I have seen very little written about our own business, frankly, that's particularly insightful. I think most reporters have little understanding of the dynamics of the whole business—what its economic underpinnings are, what the challenges are and so forth.

MSJ: *How about a particularly egregious instance of unfair coverage that you recall?*

Lawrence: On the horrifying end, on the sort of really lousy end, when this newspaper went through a re-examination of how to reach readers—which, not incidentally, is a significant challenge in our business everywhere—we ended up with a really mediocre, mocking *New York Times* story, which in this world of pack journalism that absolutely exists, sort of became the theme of the day.

MSJ: *Given that, what do you tell your staff and what would you convey to your colleagues in the news media about coverage?*

Lawrence: I'm a very old-fashioned person. I think that the values I was raised with work well in good daily newspaper journalism. I think you truly do treat people in the fashion you would want to be treated—you don't pull your punches, you're tough in your reporting, but you don't see compassion as a weakness, thoughtfulness as a weakness.

I think every reporter or editor responsible for coverage ought to be covered himself or herself. It's a wonderful object lesson.

* * *

MSJ: *On the occasions that you have been covered by the news media, how would you describe your experience of coverage overall? Has it been generally fair or unfair? For instance, what are the types of things you would discuss privately with other editors, but would rarely voice publicly?*

Geneva Overholser: The main thing that I have derived from having been covered over the years—and some articles seem to me embarrassingly *positive* and some articles seem to me unfairly negative—is that the best way for anyone who has been covered to judge coverage is as a whole. I really feel strongly that if I were to look at the coverage of me over the course of the years that I've been in the press as a whole, then I would have to say that a fairly accurate picture of me at work— or of my work—emerges.

But this raises a difficult question. What about the person who is covered one time? I think we need to learn from that to have a very powerful awareness of what the impact on an individual can be. Our sympathies really need to be with those people who are only covered once.

MSJ: *In your personal experience, can you think of a specific occasion when you were the target of unfair coverage? Can you describe it, as well as the elements that made the coverage unfair?*

Overholser: If I had been covered only in my departure from *The Des Moines Register*, and through the lens of people discovering later that David Westphal, the managing editor, and I were now married and living together in Washington, then I think I would find it unfair. The unfairness I viewed there is that journalists aren't good at nuance. We don't do subtlety. Everything has to be in black and white. If we find out some interesting thing, then it overshadows everything else.

The interesting thing in my case, and it is very interesting, is that I was in love with my managing editor—and this is *verboten*. Then, rather than think about the fact that two things might coexist, that there might be a truthfulness about all my professional statements that was as large as this other fact…it was sort of like all of the things that we say about the press: It concentrates on conflict, it likes the salacious, it tends toward the "gotcha," it wants to find out what it didn't know and then decides that that's what counts, and it doesn't take anything at face value. All those things came into play, and nothing else mattered.

And so I did find the coverage about that unfair. If I had to pick a particularly unfair article, I'd cite a front-page *Wall Street Journal* article with a drawing of me on the cover. It was amazing to me.

MSJ: *Are there any instances that stick out in your mind because of their fairness?*

Overholser: I'm sure I've been covered fairly many times, but the major stories on me have consistently either been embarrassingly glowing or incredibly dark and without a recognition of having some redeeming qualities. Or more important, it's that I did some terrible thing and therefore every good thing I might have done in my life must turn out not to be true.

While I would argue that a fairly accurate picture emerges over time, I wouldn't argue that it emerges because the preponderance of articles are fair—it emerges because you have one imbalance stacked up against another imbalance.

When I became editor of the *Register* and when the rape series won the gold medal, I was reading things that made me genuinely uncomfortable. I was reading stuff that made me think, "What's wrong with the press that it's so glowy, and why aren't the reporters in my newsroom talking to people who can't stand me?" I genuinely felt that there was a complete lack of nuance and subtlety. And I think this is what the press does. We find someone who fascinates us, a new political figure or whatever, and we write overly glowing profiles. And then it's almost as if we're embarrassed by ourselves and we have to turn on them.

MSJ: *So, from your experiences with coverage, what have you learned? What ideas would you like to convey to your colleagues about fair and unfair coverage?*

Overholser: When we've found out something about someone, we really need to think whether or not we have a responsibility to give readers a fuller picture. If we are doing something about some car dealer in town who is suddenly charged with something, don't we have an obligation to mention the many times he's been cited for community service, to give a fuller picture? Generally we think of ourselves as having done that, but I think that's one of the ways we fall down.

I find two things very disturbing that occur to me as a result of having been covered—both very favorably and unfavorably. One is that when you're being interviewed by a reporter who has a story, you can hear in that reporter's questions that he or she already has the story. You can't say, "Wait a minute, how about this?" because they've got their questions and they feel like they already know what the story is.

The other part that is particularly chilling to me is that once a story is hatched, it's as if all the herd behavior is true. The story is determined by one medium—one newspaper or one TV account. Where is the independence of one reporter as against another? We've lost it, partly through the Internet and Nexis, which afford journalists easy access to stories and quotes without doing their own investigating. People have got their story before they call you, and it's always that everyone's got the same story. No one seems to be asking whether or not they might be doing some independent reporting that would find out a more interesting story. Partly because news organizations are being consolidated and partly because of electronic reporting, I think we all feed at the same trough.

Jerry Ceppos is executive editor and senior vice president of the San Jose Mercury News.

Shelby Coffey III, is the former editor of the Los Angeles Times, U.S. News & World Report *and the* Dallas Times Herald *and a former deputy managing editor of* The Washington Post.

Max Frankel, media columnist for The New York Times Magazine, *is the former executive editor of* The New York Times.

James Hoge, a 1992–93 Media Studies Center fellow, is editor of Foreign Affairs. *He is the former publisher of the* New York Daily News *and editor and publisher of the* Chicago Sun-Times.

Dave Lawrence is publisher of The Miami Herald.

Geneva Overholser, the former editor of The Des Moines *(Iowa) Register, is ombudsman for* The Washington Post.

25

Review Essay: Meaning from the Muddle

Donald W. Shriver, Jr.

The Virtuous Journalist.
Stephen Klaidman and Tom L. Beauchamp.
New York: Oxford University Press, 1987.

Doing Ethics in Journalism:
Decision-Making in the Newsroom and in the Field.
The Poynter Institute: St. Petersburg, Fla., 1995.

News Values: Ideas for an Information Age.
Jack Fuller. Chicago: University of Chicago Press, 1996.

Media Ethics: Cases and Moral Reasoning.
Clifford G. Christians, Mark Fackler, Kim B. Rotzoll and Kathy
Brittain McKee. 5th ed. New York: Longman, 1998.

Long ago Aristotle observed that it is hard to be considered an expert in ethics because everybody seems to think that they know something about the subject. And they do. A person could not grow up in a city-state, Aristotle would say, without acquiring ethical habits. Perhaps an isolated individual can be said to be unacquainted with ethics, but the Greeks had a word for such a person: idiot.

Ethics and morality are not the same thing. Morality, in theoretical discussions, denotes the standards of behavior at work in a given society. Ethics concerns the theory behind those standards and the critical discussion of what passes as moral in our actual behavior. Under that distinction, everyone has morals, but not everyone has a theory of morals. Even so with journalists.

Most journalists I know have, deep in their conscience, a prohibition against lying when they report the news. If asked why lying is wrong for journalists, the answers are likely to be diverse: It's just wrong. It misserves the public. It undermines the profession. It will eventually lose business. It's irresponsible.

All of these statements are, in fact, the kernels of ethical theories. "Just wrong" is the classic answer of philosopher Immanuel Kant. "Bad for business, the profession and public good" takes a utilitarian, results-oriented approach. And "irresponsible" suggests a mixture of considerations that opens the discussion to circumstantial factors: If outright lying is intrinsically wrong, what about telling less than the truth? And in what circumstances might it be right, good or responsible to tell less than "the truth, the whole truth, and nothing but the truth?"

But the challenge of ethics does not end with theories. It is the *ranking* of these principles that concerns these works and most books on the ethics of journalism. Elevate any one of these ideas and you must then ask how that choice affects the importance you assign to the rest of them. If you oppose lying in the news because it is bad for business, what about those times when shading the truth appears to be good for business—as when television hypes upcoming news stories to draw viewers?

Journalists wrestle daily with the questions that occupy ethicists and theologians. All of them struggle to give order and meaning to the endless and confusing flow of human experience. If they acknowledge their common purpose, they will have much to teach each other. And, as the works reviewed here attest, they will be able to learn in a variety of settings—from the classroom to the newsroom to those private spaces where people read for knowledge and pleasure.

The best ethical advisers work by making judgments about meaning and value. Rare, however, will be the journalist who has much patience with a brand of ethical theory ensconced on the high plateau of generalities. When ethical theory rides into the busy arena of today's human events, it has to dismount from its apparent high horse and become pedestrian. That is not entirely a bad thing. The best ethical advisers—to journalists and every other professional—seek to take account of the facts, values, responsibilities and perspectives that emerge from routine perplexities. The works reviewed here offer many illustrations.

One appears at the end of *Media Ethics*, a long textbook built around 78 case studies ranging in their issues from truth and justice in newswriting, to profit, censorship, conflicting loyalties and obligations to the public. At the end is a postcript, a 79th case personal to one of the authors. He (perhaps she, there is no indication) accepts an assignment to teach a course on journalistic ethics to a group of young journalists in Uganda. There, his appreciation of the social and political supports necessary for genuine press freedom takes a sudden leap forward. "Teaching media ethics to students in countries where writers they have read sit in prison puts a different cast on classroom dialogue.... Of what good is grand ethical theory in cultures that don't reward or recognize virtue in plain clothes?"

What does journalistic "plain-clothes virtue" look like when it walks down the street? Ideal values, principles and loyalties look good on academic racks. But how, to cite two examples from *Media Ethics*, would they wear in Kampala, where the courts are subservient to a dictator? Or in California, when the *San Francisco Examiner* refused, in March 1997, to publish Stephanie Salter's column critical of the Nike company, one of the paper's income sources? When values, principles and loyalties conflict with each other in the clutch of circumstance, ethical reflection becomes serious business.

Nothing is so practical as a good theory, as psychologist Kurt Lewin has observed. Unfortunately, nothing is so practical as a bad theory, too. The ethical theory we need most would help us decide which of our values is the most valuable, and how they might all get some expression in our actual behavior.

The authors of *Media Ethics* are aware that they may drown readers in a sea of prolixity. So they begin their long volume with a sophisticated, four-dimensional model—the "Potter Box," after its Harvard inventor, Dr. Ralph Potter. The Potter Box establishes the factors that journalists should take into account when they report "the news"—facts, values, principles and loyalties—and shows how these factors interact. The Potter Box arranges these factors in a hierarchy and then sets them in motion. It begins with the facts, which for journalists are always noted or neglected according to what editors and reporters consider important or trivial news. Their reporting ought to observe certain values and ethical principles (like truth and justice). And all of this ought to be disciplined by an answer to the question: "To whom are we loyal?"

Though such sophistication may strain the patience of the average reporter or editor, this model is especially useful in the authors' insistence that all four bases should be visited and revisited in a circulating fashion. When is undercover spying, for example, a proper tactic for news gathering? For the investigation of organized crime, it may be the strategy of choice. For helping one political party undermine the credibility of another, it is highly questionable. The criterion likely to govern all these cases will be: To whose need or interest must we be primarily loyal? All of these books tend to answer "the public."

With its wide range of case studies, *Media Ethics* would be a handy book to have on any journalist's shelf for reference when she or he faces one of the issues highlighted in the book's collection of cases. Pressed as they are by the dailiness of the news business, however, reporters and editors will need sabbatical leaves if they are to ponder some of these books in a relaxed, reflective mood. Instead, were I an editor interested in developing the ethical sense of my reporters, I might set aside a couple of hours a month for small group discussions—not only of some case in these books, but of a case in the recent or remote past of journalism that merits revisiting. Were there good reasons for ignoring sex in the White House during the Kennedy administration? For focusing on it during the Clinton administration? What are the political, public costs of the change? Perhaps the most serious ethical reflection among professionals occurs when colleagues reflect on their own cases, asking the painful questions: "How could we have done it better? And what do we mean by 'better'?"

For a handy checklist of ethical guidelines and for catalyzing a lunch discussion among journalists, the Poynter Institute's video and user's guide, *Doing Ethics in Journalism*, could be very useful. It first proposes a journalistic version of the Hippocratic oath—"Seek truth...act independently...minimize harm." Then it suggests questions reporters might ask on their way to writing "responsibly." (Who will be affected? What are the other possible perspectives? What if I were the person I'm interviewing?) But the most useful piece of the Poynter schematic for journalistic ethics is its illustration of the transition from "gut reaction" ethics to observation of rules to the maturity of reflection and reasoning. At the top of this hierarchy is their assertion that "collaboration is essential." That is, check the story with your colleagues. Given the rush to deadline and competition among reporters in most newsrooms, this is rare advice. Yet, if journalism is a medium of dialogue among citizens, it seems right for the dialogue to begin in the newsroom.

In pauses to reflect, journalists, like the rest of us, are likely to find themselves reaching for some version of Jack Fuller's "mental moorings," a nice metaphor for the concepts that push the discussion of ethics along the line: "Free press, yes, but freedom *for what and for whom*?" Both Fuller's *News Values* and Klaidman and Beauchamp's *The Virtuous Journalist* are replete with philosophic responses to such umbrella questions. Fuller, president of the Tribune Publishing Co. and a former editor of the *Chicago Tribune*, Klaidman an experienced reporter on international affairs *for The New York Times* and *The Washington Post*, Beauchamp a professor of philosophy at Georgetown University. Were I trying to prove to some of my own academic colleagues that "journalism" is not a synonym for shallow thinking, I would refer them to these two books. Journalists, too, can write learned books with dozens of references to "truth" and "fact" and with sprinkles of quotations from philosophers John Rawls, Sissela Bok and Karl Popper.

A reading of *The Virtuous Journalist*, which is rich in ethical ideas, prompts the following sort of maxims that journalists should carry into every assignment. Respect the complexity of circumstances, even when you have to simplify them. Treat people as persons, not things or hooks. Ask how you would like to be reported on were you being visited by a reporter. Remember that the truth about fellow humans can seldom be reduced to what is newsworthy about them. Consider the follow-ups necessary to correct a first story. If you are writing "the first draft of history," will future historians thank you or contradict you?

The most common answer to the "what" of good journalism in these books, is "truth." The most common answer to the "for whom" is "the public." Many an ethical tension arises in these pages between fairness to truth, fairness to individuals, and fairness to public need. Fuller, Klaidman and Beauchamp's respective treatments of these three relationships illuminate ethical issues that face not just journalists but every communicator. And who, after all, is not a communicator?

Is the truth the interesting or the significant? Fuller begins his book affirming that both are norms for determining what is news. "Significance and interest provide separate bases for calling an event or piece of information news, and either may be sufficient." People may yawn over the Salt II talks and wake up to Michael Jordan's short career in baseball, but both belong in the paper. In the beginning of *News Values*, Fuller does not focus much on the tension between these two norms, and I think him rather complacent with this "both/and" rule. One could wish that he explored them in connection with the recent vast coverage of O.J Simpson, Princess Diana and sex in the White House. In the spring of 1995, when I was teaching at the Columbia Graduate School of Journalism, one could detect the professional chagrin of a class of print journalists at the proportion of public attention to the Simpson trial promoted by television. By the same token, the spectacle of TV news anchors ordered back to Washington at the first stirrings of the

Clinton/Starr/Lewinsky scandal, and thus cutting short their coverage of the papal visit to Cuba, does little credit to the profession. Much to his credit, Tom Brokaw went outside the world of television to protest this executive decision in the op-ed page of the *Times*. Still, these cases make it harder for the public to draw the line between "responsible" journalism and the tabloids. These few months into the 1998 White House scandal, the majority of the public seems abashed at media attention to these events while vast issues of war, peace and mass murder simmer on the back pages.

Later in the book, Fuller is much clearer about the tension between intrinsic importance of and public interest in the news. "Here is the tension: A newspaper that fails to reflect its community deeply will not succeed. But a newspaper that does not challenge its community's values and preconceptions will lose respect for failing to provide the honesty and leadership that newspapers are expected to offer." In their discovery that a minority position, once maligned editorially, is actually right, editors may have some repenting to do. This is an advanced form of ethical consciousness. As Psalm 15:4 puts it, righteous persons are those who "swear to their own hurt." Much to his credit, Fuller then concedes that "the behavior of many newspapers—including the *Tribune*—during the civil rights movement and the McCarthy era provides a lesson uncomfortably close to home." Good for Fuller—he included his own paper.

In the what and how of their news stories and editorials about unpopular movements, newspapers can reach for the standards of the Hebrew prophets, who knew that popularity often signals untruth. Unless they are driven by something more than market forces—including the market of public opinion—the media will lose one of the principal arguments for the ethical justification of a free press: that it gives minorities, including the minority of one, the freedom to get a hearing.

Is fairness to persons a combination of behavior plus empathy? ABC News' Jeff Greenfield once observed that the American press was slow to tune into the civil rights movement in the 1950s because its reporters were not interested in things going on in the basements of African-American churches. Journalism ordinarily attends to what happens above ground. But for reporting the news, behaviorism is as poor a psychological theory as social determinism. Most of us are interested not only in what others do but why they do it. Nevertheless, in the classic "Ws" of news reporting, the why is often the most neglected. Rare is the person among us who, having been "covered" by the press, has resisted the thought, "I wish they had probed a little more deeply." Motives, meanings and their clashes *inside* our personhood are ingredients of being *understood*. Understanding belongs in the news, as does the assumption of free will. When humans do something, they are likely to have had the ability to do something else. Law, ethics and journalism all have a central stake in that presumption.

What does it mean to be fair to the whole of another human being? Fuller rightly exhibits great interest in this issue. In doing so he expands the duty of reporters toward an ethically more serious matter than "fairness." Says he: "...fairness is a poor choice of words to describe a journalist's discipline.... The ideal of intellectual honesty, tested by the Golden Rule, offers a much surer guide." This is an astonishing concession on his part, for it puts the journalist on notice that he ought to be first cousin to the anthropologist Clifford Geertz, professor of social science at the Institute for Advanced Study in Princeton, New Jersey, who seeks to understand the members of another culture from inside its own presuppositions, habits and norms. This is empathy, in which we reach understanding despite all our differences. To understand all is neither to forgive all nor to justify all; it is rather to take into account the reasons—ordinary, exotic, right or wrong—that people take with them into their personal and social behaviors. Taking account of these fuzzy, often invisible realities is the most difficult part of the journalistic trade. It is empirically demanding and ethically essential.

One could wish, for example, that in the long seventy years of the existence of the Soviet Union, American journalists had helped their public more faithfully to see Americans as the Soviets saw us. Had we understood better the historic Russian paranoia at the threat of invasion, we might have calmed the Cold War sooner, and we would know why Russians fear the expansion of NATO to their own borders. Fuller, though, claims that newspapers must be primarily loyal to the interests and needs of their national publics. In our emerging global era, this seems very short-sighted on his part. Even from the standpoint of American self-interest, it is vital for Americans to learn, in the words of the Scottish poet Robert Burns, to "see ourselves as others see us." Perhaps Fuller would agree that it is in the interest of every nation to take account of how others see them.

If the rule of empathy applies to whole cultures and countries, it is equally mandatory for news about individuals. *Media Ethics* treats a number of cases in which the media promoted or exploded stereotypes of certain "classes" of people, such as gays and the homeless. As any religious minister or social worker knows, most of us ordinarily resist entering deeply into the trials and tribulations of other people. It is one thing to stand by as a curious observer, quite another to *understand*. Moreover, in a world where the list of potential news stories seems to be infinite, what kind of stories should journalists try to understand—and when? Says Fuller: "The journalist sees his role as informing people of what they need to know in order to be functioning citizens, whether they want to know it or not. He takes it as his primary duty to tell the truth about important things."

But this is a momentous ethical assertion, implying that the journalist knows, or can come to know, what is good, right and important for the public to know. Some journalists will shrink from this bold assertion, and they will need to read all the Fuller book to decide if he is on target and responsible or off base and paternalistic in drawing this bottom line for his ethics. It's as close to a dominant, controversial, overarching issue as any in this cluster of books.

What does the public "need" to know? The composing of any news story, Fuller notes, requires a story line, an organization of complex facts and a focus that somehow adds up to "meaning." Something in the story holds it together, defining its significance to both the journalist and the reader. Editorial writers practice this art most overtly; they intend to sum up complex events and tell the public what they mean.

Editorial writers may be wrong, of course, in their interpretations of events. But if they do not make the attempt, how can uninformed readers make up their minds? We want our journalists to try to make sense of things, says Fuller. "The profusion of choices presented to people will make the function of those who help make those choices more secure, not less. When people can get any information available anywhere, they will need ways to simplify the selection process. They will need to establish time-saving habits. And they will need ways to create meaning from the muddle."

Philosophers have long proposed two tests of "truth"—correspondence and coherence. In journalists' terms, that means getting the facts straight and writing a story that makes sense of things. Plainly, Fuller opts for coherence as the overriding test of journalistic truth. His book is an editor's impressive effort to combat postmodern views of human values, with their utter relativism and their inability to cohere around any stable notions of the good, the true and the beautiful. Neither editors nor reporters, he is sure, can sustain their own morale or the morale of the public if they are nourished only by the belief that "nothing is true or false but thinking makes it so." There are truths, values, principles and loyalties without which neither persons nor societies can survive. Postmodernism kills not only some stories, but journalism itself.

Humans, including reporters, "do believe in things—even in the things they criticize," such as their country, which is Fuller's "first loyalty." One wonders if Fuller's demand for coherence is compatible with this patriotic center of loyalty. Does Fuller see room, as a hurried journalist in search of meaning, for something like loyalty to human beings as such? To other countries, too? When there is a decline of reader interest in world news (such as seems now to be happening in the United States) is the editor of the *Tribune* bound to keep telling readers, in headlines, what they need to know? Including what the citizens of other lands need *us* to know?

However inconsistent, Fuller makes this his virtual statement of faith: "Regardless of what the radical skeptics argue, people still passionately believe in meaning. They want the whole picture, not just part of it.... They are tired of polarized discussion, the 'McLaughlin Group' model of public discourse.... [Therefore] the acceptance of modest opinion in news accounts provides context and coherence and communicates meaning."

That, says Fuller, is exactly what the Internet will never provide us. Neither will any interactive news medium that simply gives citizens what they choose to know. Civic discourse, in particular, thrives not just on what every individual wants to know but on what individuals have to tell each other. A proper newspaper does not offer a self-chosen clipping service, Fuller writes, but "a window onto the world.... People come to a newspaper craving a unifying human presence.... They want a synthesizer who can pull a world together from the fragments."

No reader of words like these can fail to recognize their kinship with the lifeview of *religion*, and some will want accordingly to raise a "Beware" sign over the Fuller book. The former *Tribune* editor is frank to concede that "those words hearken back to a kind of old-time newspaper religion, one that believes that knowledge [or meaningful truth] gives people power." There is indeed something very old-fashioned-American about such language. It reminds one of de Tocqueville's observation that early European Americans advanced into the forests of the West armed principally with "a Bible, an ax, and a newspaper." In Fuller's view, the American public is bereft of the kind of unifying vision of meaning that many of our ancestors found in the Bible. In that absence of meaning, the media have an awesome responsibility for guiding us moderns through the wilderness of an information-surfeited age.

So, by the end of *News Values* we stand with a journalist on a different sort of frontier: between ethics and religion. As one theologian, I am frank to confess that I am both attracted and repelled by the Fuller version of the mission of the media. Religion stands for something of permanent value: meanings that promise to bring coherence out of the muddle of things. Many reporters and editors are understandably afraid to measure their work by such a high standard. Yet it really is possible and necessary, as Kant argues, to bring enduring order and focus to the streams of consciousness in which all of us are in danger of drowning. Reason meets religion—and journalism—at the place where some "ultimate concern," in theologian Paul Tillich's phrase, searches the sky for a north star. Sociologist Peter Berger speaks of the "sacred canopy" that societies affirm for distinguishing between things of lesser and greater importance.

In the sobriety of their sense of professional competence, most writers in these books shy away from any claim to supplying their readers with the final truth about anything. But Fuller is onto a mood in modern America that asks its communicators to come clean on what they believe about the meaning of their work in the context of the meaning of their life. Who the reporter is influences what she writes. We can still enjoy our pluralism and our right to argue with the ultimate concerns of our neighbors and our publicists. But we ought not to dispute the obligation of leadership—in any sector—to tell us explicitly, from time to time, about their own mental moorings.

This is bound to be a discomforting challenge to the ordinary canons of "objective" journalism. It is hard enough for journalists to feel comfortable about discussing abstract ethical principles. But to identify which among those principles have some quality of religious ultimacy? There's the rub—an abrasive one for most.

When journalists turn to writing books, they are likely to probe some of the depths present in all these books. Ordinary newswriting does not have to shout, "See what values impel me to write it this way!" But values and beliefs do surface in the luxuries of book writing. During a year of study with practicing journalists at the Freedom Forum Media Studies Center, I chanced to talk one day with Terry Anderson, then writing *Den of Lions*, the book about his seven-year imprisonment in Lebanon. "It's hard to write about it," he said, "because I have to include a description of my feelings, including my grappling with religion. It's not what the AP accustomed me to write about."

Whether we call it religion or just ethics, the life we call human seems to be attached to something of such great value as to be worthy of the confession, "Here I stand," as Martin Luther put it. Fuller says he once asked Eppie Lederer (the real "Ann Landers") "whether she wrote in her own voice or someone else's. 'I write,' she said, 'in the voice of a person as good as I would like to be.'"

Public dispute about better and worse there must be, for collaborative reflection is likely to produce more ethical wisdom than a single intelligence can muster. That is what journalism professor James Carey means when he says that "journalism and democracy are names for the same thing." But the good we have to offer one another may have to include our respective visions of the best. Journalists and the rest of us will enhance our service to each other if we are free to voice those visions.

Donald W. Shriver, Jr., a 1992–94 Media Studies Center fellow, is president emeritus and William E. Dodge Professor of Applied Christianity at Union Theological Seminary.

For Further Reading

Benjamin, Burton. *Fair Play: CBS, General Westmoreland, and How a Television Documentary Went Wrong.* New York: Harper & Row, 1988.

Black, Jay, Bob Steele and Ralph D. Barney. *Doing Ethics in Journalism.* Boston: Allyn and Bacon, 1995.

Callahan, Daniel, William Green, Bruce Jennings and Martin Linsky. *Congress and the Media: The Ethical Connection.* Hastings-on-Hudson, N.Y.: Hastings Center, 1985.

Christians, Clifford G., P. Mark Fackler and John P. Ferre. *Good News: Social Ethics and the Press.* New York: Oxford University Press, 1993.

Cohen, Elliot D. *Philosophical Issues in Journalism.* New York: Oxford University Press, 1992.

Dennis, Everette E., Donald M. Gilmor and Theodore L. Glasser. *Media Freedom and Accountability.* New York: Greenwood Press, 1989.

Elliott, Deni. *Responsible Journalism.* Beverly Hills, Calif.: Sage, 1986.

Fuller, Jack. *News Values: Ideas for an Information Age.* Chicago: University of Chicago Press, 1996.

Goldstein, Tom. *News at Any Cost: How Journalists Compromise Their Ethics to Shape the News.* New York: Simon & Schuster, 1985.

Goodwin, Gene, and Ron F. Smith. *Groping for Ethics in Journalism.* Ames, Iowa: Iowa State University Press, 1994.

Gordon, A. David, John M. Kittross and Carol Reuss. *Controversies in Media Ethics.* White Plains, N.Y.: Longman, 1996.

Gross, Larry, John Stuart Katz and Jay Ruby. *Image Ethics: the Moral Rights of Subjects in Photographs, Film, and Television.* New York: Oxford University Press, 1988.

Hausman, Carl. *Crisis of Conscience: Perspectives on Journalism Ethics.* New York: HarperCollins, 1992.

Isaacs, Norman E. *Untended Gates: The Mismanaged Press.* New York: Columbia University Press, 1986.

Klaidman, Stephen, and Tom L. Beauchamp. *The Virtuous Journalist.* New York: Oxford University Press, 1987.

Knowlton, Steven R., and Patrick R. Parsons. *The Journalist's Moral Compass: Basic Principles.* Westport, Conn.: Praeger, 1995.

Lambeth, Edmund B. *Committed Journalism: An Ethic for the Profession.* Bloomington, Ind.: Indiana University Press, 1986.

Leigh, Robert D., ed. *A Free and Responsible Press by The Commission on Freedom of the Press.* Chicago: University of Chicago Press, 1947 (Midway Reprint 1974).

Levy, Philip H. *The Press Council: History, Procedure and Case.* New York: St. Martin's Press, 1967.

Merrill, John C. *Journalism Ethics: Philosophical Foundations for News Media.* New York: St. Martin's Press, 1997.

————. *Existential Journalism.* Ames, Iowa: Iowa State University Press, 1996.

Munson, Eve Stryker, and Catherine A. Warren, eds. *James Carey: A Critical Reader.* Minneapolis: University of Minnesota Press, 1997.

Shaw, David. Press Watch: *A Provocative Look at How Newspapers Report the News.* New York: Macmillan, 1984.

Simpson, Alan K. *Right in the Old Gazoo: A Lifetime of Scrapping with the Press.* New York: William Morrow, 1997.

Weaver, Paul H. *News and the Culture of Lying.* New York: Free Press, 1994.

Index